*Civil War in Pictures*

*Civil*
*in*

# *War*
# *Pictures*

## by FLETCHER PRATT

GARDEN CITY BOOKS,
Garden City, New York

# PREFACE

This is a book about the Civil War by the people who saw it and lived it. It is a compilation, mainly from the files of *Harper's Weekly*, but also with a good deal of material from *Frank Leslie's Illustrated Newspaper*, of on-the-spot reports and drawings of what happened during the greatest of American conflicts and of the popular conception of the importance of the events of the war.

The Brady photographs have become justly celebrated for their contemporary delineation of war details and scenes. But the technical equipment of photography in 1861-65 did not permit anything but time exposures, and there was no means of reproducing a photograph directly. Therefore very few participants in the Civil War ever saw a Brady photograph. It had to be reduced to a drawing and the drawing reduced to a woodcut before it got in the papers.

The two weeklies provided the main contemporary pictorial coverage, and it was only very rarely that anyone got any other idea of what the war looked like beyond what the weeklies printed. Since pictures of any kind were rarely published, there was then, as there is today, a very genuine desire to know what things *looked* like while they were happening. The result was the artist-correspondents. A few of them, most especially Winslow Homer, went on to other things after the war. But mostly they were painstaking reporters, even more so than the men who reported the war in type.

On the whole they did an extremely good job. At the outset of the war, they had certain preconceived notions —for example, that horses gallop with their feet out in front and behind, in a series of jumps like a dog or rabbit —but these began to disappear as a result of direct observation, and one of the interesting things about this collection is the steady increase in realism.

The accompanying text is also largely from the two weeklies concerned, with such comment as seems necessary. The most interesting thing about it is the constant interplay of misestimates and accurate insights that have been fully confirmed by the judgment of history; and probably the next most interesting thing is how much the historians have missed, how different the emphasis was while people were living through the events the artists and correspondents were setting down.

It is a partisan book; it could not be anything else. There were no illustrated weeklies published in Richmond or Montgomery or Charleston.

Many of the quotations have been sensibly abridged, but an effort has been made to keep their essential flavor.

*Civil War in Pictures*

Charleston housetops during the bombardment of Sumter

The war has now begun in earnest. The secession of Virginia, and the attempts of the rebels to seize the Arsenal at Harper's Ferry and the Navy-yard at Norfolk; the investment of Fort Pickens; the threatened seizure of the Federal Capital by the rebels; the murder of Massachusetts men in Baltimore—these facts explain the situation without further comment.

It is not now a question of slavery or anti-slavery. It is not even a question of Union or disunion. The question simply is whether Northern men will fight.

8

This was how *Harper's Weekly* introduced the Civil War to its readers; and at the time this was the question uppermost in most men's minds. Nearly a million and a half voters, most of them in the North, had cast their ballots for Stephen A. Douglas, in the understanding that the South was right in principle if not in method; and Horace Greeley had declared from his forum of the pro-Lincoln *Tribune* that it were best to "Let the erring sisters go" when the news of secession came. Would the North fight?

The answer came with the news of the firing on Sumter and Lincoln's call to arms. Rarely in our history has there been such an outburst of enthusiasm so spontaneous. In Wisconsin a judge and jury walked from the court to enlist together; in Boston the bells rang all day; before night 3000 men had joined the colors; in New York, Union Square was jammed with a monster mass meeting, and the 7th Regiment marched down Broadway through a tempest of cheering. "It was worth a life, that march," wrote Theodore Winthrop, who was to give exactly a life for it in battle not long later.

"The Rising of the North" bulked larger in contemporary accounts than in most of those written since; but there was some question whether Maryland was a Northern or Southern state, and the matter came to a head with the arrival of the 6th Massachusetts, en route to Washington. The tracks were not continuous; they had to debark at the Philadelphia station,

The march of the 7th New York

The attack on the 6th Massachusetts in Baltimore

take horse cars across town, and another train to their destination. A mob gathered, cheering for secession and Jeff Davis. *Harper's Weekly* says:

"Six of the cars had succeeded in passing on their way before the crowd were able to accomplish their purpose of barricading the track, which they now began to effect by placing large, heavy anchors across the rails."

As the soldiers debarked and it became visible that comparatively few of them carried arms, the mob became bolder; soon there were stones flying, then clubs, then a revolver shot. The soldiers presented arms once and fired a volley; but now they had to fight their way through. After they had reached the station the mob got completely out of hand, fired the railroad station, and ran locomotives into the stream. For the time being Maryland refused to allow more Northern troops to cross her soil or at least to pass through Baltimore.

The sensation the affair made in the North was nothing as to the sensation in Washington. All telegraph wires were down; people began packing furniture for flight in case the Confederates came, and even some government archives were boxed for shipment. But the Confederates did not come; instead it was the New York 7th and a Rhode Island battery, in by water from Annapolis. And Mr. Allen Pinkerton the detective had so thoroughly infiltrated the pro-secession groups in Baltimore that when things quieted down he was able to lay his hands on most of the mob leaders.

Norfolk was one of the largest U. S. navy yards. As soon as Virginia seceded, it was evident that it could not be held, and Commodore McCauley in charge was ordered to get all ships ready for sea. He was an old man and not very energetic; his reply was that there were no crews for the big sailing sloops, and the engines of the steam frigate *Merrimack*, one of the finest ships in the navy, were not in order.

Says *Harper's Weekly:*

On Saturday evening the *Pawnee* arrived with 200 volunteers and 100 marines and at once the officers and crew went to the Navy-yard and spiked the guns, and threw the shot and small arms into the river. A party of officers meanwhile was going through the different buildings and ships, distributing waste and turpentine and laying a train to blow up the Dry Dock. They were engaged in this work until two o'clock, when the train was fired. At three o'clock the *Yankee,* to the Captain of which, Charles Germain, much credit is due, came along and took the *Cumberland* in tow, the *Pawnee* taking the lead.

The burning of the ships at Norfolk: *United States,* Tug *Yankee, Cumberland, Merrimac, Pawnee, Pennsylvania*

Landing of the relief expedition to Fort Pickens

The conflagration took *United States,* Stephen Decatur's old cruiser, and *Pennsylvania,* once the largest wooden warship in the world, with everything that would burn in the buildings. But the Confederates were left with the hull of *Merrimack,* of which they were to make immense use later; and also with over 500 heavy cannon, which were used in most of the Mississippi and coastal forts.

In contemporary eyes, Fort Pickens in Pensacola harbor was fully as important as Sumter, and in some contemporary eyes more so. When the expedition that failed to relieve the latter place was fitting out, its flagship was intended to be the powerful side-wheel frigate *Powhatan,* but Secretary of State Seward, who was then still under the impression that he was running the country, procured an order which sent her to Pickens instead. Her gun power and the reinforcements she brought discouraged the Confederates from any idea of opening fire from Fort McRae, across the harbor, and when Washington learned what had happened, it decided to follow through and send more troops.

*Harper's Weekly:*

The *Illinois,* with reinforcements, arrived at midnight on Friday the 19th, and her troops were landed the next morning. Seven of the horses were lost. The forage and light artillery were landed simultaneously with the horses. On the 18th the landing of the general cargo of heavy and light ammunition, provisions, etc., etc., was fairly commenced. The position of the *Powhatan* and *Brooklyn* was such that their guns could sweep Santa Rosa Island and prevent a landing from the main land.

The Confederates never did take Pickens; in fact they were driven from their own positions in the harbor after a furious artillery duel.

Among conflicts the Civil War is remarkable and practically unique in getting off to an extremely slow start. After the firing on Sumter there was some sporadic fighting in Missouri and a minor, scrambling contact at Big Bethel in Virginia; there were a couple of minor battles in what is now West Virginia, but then nothing at all on land until Bull Run, near the end of July, and then again nothing until nearly a year of the war had run.

In the meantime, in camps around Washington and throughout the North, men were learning to be soldiers — or at least learning the minor arts involved, such as how to carry, load, and fire a musket, how to march in step, and the meaning of the words of command. Most of these amateur soldiers were also learning about how to live in common with other men, messing together and sharing tents; a few were learning how to live in the open, though this was not particularly necessary in many Northern regiments which came from pioneering country.

This was not true of Daniel Sickles' "Excelsior Brigade," raised by that Tammany Congressman from his office on Broadway and, of course, commanded by him. He was the man who shot Philip Barton Key for seducing his wife, and was acquitted through the ministrations of the future Secretary of War, E. M. Stanton; it does not appear to have diminished his popularity in New York, and he had no trouble in filling out the brigade.

Most of the formations had names in those days, and there was a wild profusion of uniforms, matched only by the numbers of types of weapons. Sickles' brigade was an exception to both cases; his men wore the prescribed uniform, and being a Tammany politician he saw to it that they were well equipped. When the camp was near home territory, it was usual for curious citizens to make a holiday

Bivouac of General Sickles' brigade at the Red House, Harlem

out of turning out to watch drills and evolutions, and even to stay around to see the eating habits of those peculiar individuals, the soldiers.

Correspondents and artists during the early days of the Civil War enjoyed a freedom of movement and reporting that would appall a modern army. Thus William H. Russell, the famous correspondent of the London *Times,* was able to travel throughout the South, meeting not only politicians but generals; and the latter had no hesitation whatever about showing him their camps and fortifications and discussing everything that was going on. More remarkable still to a modern mind, they made no objection to his printing anything he saw or heard.

The newspapers, at least in the early days of the war, made espionage practically unnecessary.

This freedom was to some extent limited in the South by an almost morbid fear of espionage. In most cities there were Vigilance Committees, unofficial counterespionage groups, who made it their business to keep track of strangers. Allen Pinkerton, who really was an espionage agent, has related several clashes with them, but he usually talked his way out without too much difficulty.

One of correspondent Russell's companions on his tour of the South was a Mr. Theodore Davis, the *Harper's Weekly* artist, who made not the slightest secret of working for a Northern paper. But he ran into a Vigilance Committee at Memphis, and then:

Our artist, Mr. Davis, met with an unpleasant adventure on his return from New Orleans. On his arrival at Memphis, Tennessee, he was waited upon by the Vigilance Committee, who inquired, after the fashion of these bodies, who he was, where he came from, what he was doing, where he was going, and whether he didn't need any hanging. Having obtained answers to these various queries, the Committee then proceeded to inspect Mr. Davis's trunk, which they overhauled with commendable thoroughness. Finding at the bottom of the trunk a number of sketches made for us, they examined them minutely, and each member, by way of remembering Mr. Davis, pocketed two or three of the most striking.

As early as the Battle of Bull Run, on July 21, 1861, the field artists were doing something more than the conventional long lines of men marching or charging as though they were marionettes. The reporting was nearly as sophisticated. *Harper's Weekly* dealt with Bull Run thus:

The grand advance movement of the Union army into Virginia took place last week. General M'Dowell, with his staff, left Arlington on the 16th, with nearly his whole force of some 60,000 men, at half past three o'clock. The brigade of General Louis Blenker, comprising the Eighth and Twenty-ninth Regiments New York Volunteers, the Garibaldi Guard, and the Twenty-fourth Regiment Pennsylvania Volunteers, formed the advance column of the grand army.

The Vigilance Committee at Memphis, Tennessee, robbing our special artist of his sketches

Battle at Bull's Run, Virginia, fought on Sunday, July 21

The rebels evacuated Fairfax Court House and Centreville as our troops advanced, falling back on Bull's Run and Manassas Gap. A reconnoissance by General Tyler of the batteries at the former place, on the 19th, developed the enemy in great strength; and on Sunday morning, 21st, General M'Dowell attacked them there. These batteries were taken by our troops, and the whole day was spent in hard fighting. At 2 P.M. it seemed that we had carried all the points attacked. But just then General Johnson brought up his army in support of Beauregard, a panic suddenly broke out in our army, and it retreated on Centreville, Fairfax and lastly on Washington, with considerable loss. Jeff Davis is said to have commanded the enemy in person.

Aside from the matter of emphasis — a minor engagement at Carthage, Missouri, gets four times as much space—and the error about Jeff Davis this is not bad spot reporting. It is followed in the same column by another item of considerable future importance:

General M'Clellan, whose able management of the campaign in Western Virginia is worthy of all praise, has been called to Washington to take command of the Army of the Potomac. His presence there will no doubt inspire confidence in the men. General M'Dowell will probably resume his former position as General of brigade. Brigadier-General Rosecrans, who so gallantly won the Battle of Rich Mountain, is to succeed General M'Clellan in command of the Upper Potomac. General William S. Rosencranz is a native of Ohio and a West Point Officer, having entered the Military Academy in 1838.

In the following week the periodical was on the ball again with an editorial headed "The Lesson of Defeat":

If we are true to ourselves, the disaster of the 21st July will prove a benefit rather than an injury. It will teach us in the first place, and not only us, but those also who have in charge the national interests at this crisis, that this war must be prose-

cuted on scientific principles, and that popular clamor must not be suffered to override the dictates of experience and the rules of strategy. We have the best evidence to prove that the march to Bull Run, and the fight there, were both undertaken against the judgment of Lieutenant-General Scott, and solely in deference to the popular craving for action which owed its origin and main virulence to the New York *Tribune*. The wretched result must serve as a warning for the future.

Again. The detailed accounts of the retreat from Bull Run prove that a very large proportion of our militia officers failed in their duty on that occasion. This is no matter of surprise. In selecting company and even field officers, our militiamen often attach more weight to wealth and political or social influence than to bravery or soldierly aptitude. Very many commissions are won by intrigue. It was to be expected that they would rather lead than check a panic. This radical flaw in our military system must be corrected. Bull Run must rid us of cowardly or imbecile colonels, majors and captains. Better offend a thousand ambitious candidates for military rank than have another flight led by colonels, majors and captains.

The system of elective officers was never quite done away with, but things might have gone a good deal better if it had. In fact, history has had very little to add to this on-the-spot verdict, and it is impressive to find heads so thoroughly screwed on the right way at a time when it was easy to go wrong. One wonders if the editorials written after Pearl Harbor will read as well ninety years from the time they were written.

As early as April, 1861, James B. Eads, the wealthy St. Louis salvage master, went to Washington with plans for an ironclad gunboat to control the Mississippi. After some complex double-shuffling, this resulted in Commander John Rodgers of the navy being sent West. He doubted the efficacy of armor and completely rejected Eads' ideas, but he purchased three river steamers at Cincinnati, had them cut down and made into warships by sheathing them in five inches of oak on a plan of his own. They became the *Lexington, Tyler,* and *Conestoga* and gave good service all through the war, but the carpentry on them was so bad that they spent about a third of their time being repaired.

In August the first pictures of the most-publicized general of the war, George B. McClellan, began to appear. *Harper's Weekly* saluted him with an account of his bravery in the Mexican War, for which he was brevetted first lieutenant and then captain, and went on:

He introduced the bayonet exercise into the army and translated and adapted a manual which has since become a textbook. During the summer and fall of 1851 he superintended the construction of Fort Delaware. He was a member of the commission which went to the seat of war in the Crimea and in Northern Russia. Major McClellan's report on the Organization of European Armies and the Operations of War, a quarto volume embodying the result of his observations in the Crimea, greatly enhanced his reputation as a scientific soldier.

With the other biographical details the source of this account seems to have been McClellan himself, and it is thoroughly characteristic of him, because only about half-true. He did translate a French bayonet manual, but bayonet drill had been practiced in the U. S. Army since the Revolution; he did write a book about the Crimean tour, but it was one almost nobody read.

In this stage of the war the freedom of artists to cross the lines was still unlimited, and it surprised no one to see pictures of a Confederate encampment in a Northern paper. After Bull Run the Confederates began building

Gunboats fitting out at Cincinnati, Ohio, for government service on the Mississippi

field works at Manassas, the site of the battle, and the reports on them said they were very formidable. These reports, like those describing the enormous numbers of the Confederate Army at the place, reached McClellan through the Pinkerton detectives, and contributed in no small measure to his reluctance to attack. But when he did move toward Manassas late in the next spring, on the news that the rebels were evacuating the place, it was discovered that most of the guns were "Quakers," i.e., painted logs; and that the trench-digging had been done more to keep the Southern soldiers busy than from any serious purpose in fortifying.

Quite early in the war it became evident that the Fugitive Slave Law would be inoperative against slaves who reached the Union lines, and a trickle began in that direction. The problem was under what legal theory

Major General McClellan, U.S.A.

The 4th South Carolina Regiment working in the trenches at night at Manassas Junction

19

Stampede of slaves from Hampton to Fortress Monroe

they were to be regarded; if they were property, they ought to be impounded and held for the duration or until the loyalty of their owners was determined. This problem remained in the background until Ben Butler, commanding Fortress Monroe, decided to abandon an outpost position at Hampton, where a not inconsiderable number of refugees had gathered.

Suddenly faced with a number of refugees that demanded a solution of the problem, Butler evolved the theory of treating them as contraband of war, a term previously reserved for military goods in transit on the high seas. After this every escaped slave was a "contraband" and every forward move of the Union armies brought a flood of them.

When Lincoln proclaimed the blockade of the 3000 miles of Southern coast, the U. S. Navy had exactly eight ships in commission in home waters. A giant shipbuilding program was launched; but meanwhile the legal requirements of blockade had to be met, and almost anything that

would float and carry a gun was bought up and hastily armed for service in the blockade. There resulted the "soap-box navy," one of the strangest collections of marine knickknacks that ever sailed the seas, hastily armed with whatever guns were available. It included small freighters and large harbor tugs (most tugs were side-wheelers for better turning) and even ferryboats from New York and Boston harbors. The last proved unexpectedly and particularly useful when the attacks on the coast of Georgia and the Carolinas began. They could penetrate rivers and the narrow channels of the sounds and return without having to turn around. All the ships of the soap-box navy were of wood, none had any armor, and some were of the flimsiest character. But the work of arming them and getting them to sea in time to establish a blockade that would be recognized as legal by Britain was carried through at a pace that makes it one of the great unsung industrial efforts of the war. George D. Morgan of New York was the man chiefly re-

BARKS ARTHUR, BRAZELERO, AMANDA, AND GEM OF THE SEAS.

TUGS SATELLITE AND PUTNAM.

PROPELLERS HALE, AND STARS & STRIPES

STEAMERS AUGUSTA, JAMES ADGER, FLORIDA, AND VALLEY CITY

PREPARING MERCHANT VESSELS FOR THE
# BLOCKADE.

The fleet in line of battle at Hatteras

22

sponsible; of course, he was denounced in and investigated by Congress.

While the armies were doing little but train for the combats to come, the navy decided to seize some of the outlying islands along the Southern coast, which would both ease the problem of the blockade by providing forward bases and afford access to the inland sounds lying behind. The first expedition was launched against Hatteras Inlet on August 28, with troops under Ben Butler and a fleet under Commodore Silas Stringham.

There were two forts on opposite sides of the entrance. A landing was made on the sand spit below one of them, but that part of the operation was a failure. All the boats stove in in the surf, most of the powder was wetted and there were no provisions at all. The men dined that night on sheep caught along the shore and toasted over driftwood fires on the ends of bayonets.

With the fleet it was otherwise. Stringham had two big steam frigates, among the most powerful warships in the world, a paddle-wheel frigate, a sailing sloop, and three gunboats, giving him nearly 70 heavy guns in line.

At ten o'clock the *Wabash* fired the first gun, the eleven-inch shell striking near the battery and bursting with tremendous force. The battery, which was of sand covered with turf and mounting five long thirty-twos, instantly returned the fire, the shot falling short.

The cannonading on our part was incessant, and the air was filled with the hum and explosion of flying shells; but the enemy did not return the fire with any regularity, the battery being too hot for them, from the explosion of shells that dropped in at the rate of half a dozen a minute.

The fort held out under this for one day and part of another, but when an 11-inch pierced the bomb-proof shelter and exploded near the magazine, a white flag went up.

The bivouac fire at the outposts of our army on the Potomac

The grand review. "Taken from the Roof of the Almshouse"

The Army of the Potomac. Scene in camp after evening parade

It was the general opinion of naval men before this time that wooden ships could not deal successfully with forts ashore. Hatteras introduced a new element into the situation; it was only necessary to bring enough guns of great power and long range to bear, and the advantage of the forts disappeared. It set off a chain reaction of expeditions against the Southern coast.

Whatever else may be said of General McClellan, he had few equals either at drilling troops or gaining their affection; and he loved to exhibit the products of his skill in reviews. This one, held on October 8, was reported thus:

General M'Clellan reviewed a portion of the cavalry and artillery on this side of the Potomac today, on the broad plain east of the Capitol. Fifty-five hundred cavalry, drawn up by squadrons and regiments on the left, and eighteen batteries, each by itself, on the right, awaited the General, whose arrival with his staff was announced by salute about 12½ o'clock. After riding rapidly along the line, he took a position on a gentle rise of land. The artillery first, guns and caissons in battery line, swept by, followed by the cavalry. Among the batteries, none received more praise than that from Massachusetts, which arrived only two days ago. There were five batteries from Pennsylvania and three regular —112 guns in all—under command of General Barry, Chief of Artillery. Nearly four times as many were reviewed as on the previous occasion. General M'Clellan expressed himself more than satisfied. He noticed a marked improvement. The display of artillery was particularly fine, the guns, horses, and men being in the best condition. In many squadrons of the cavalry all the horses were of one color, which will be universally the case as soon as General Stoneman, Chief of Cavalry, can arrange it. The President and Mrs. Lincoln, Secretary and Assistant-Secretary Seward, Generals Blenker, M'Dowell, Sickles, Hooker, and Porter were present.

In the march that ended at Bull Run, Mr. Russell, the English correspondent, made most particular note

25

of the poor appearance of the Union artillery, and the wild variety of calibers it exhibited. But a little more than two months later things had already begun to change. The factories of Pittsburgh were turning out guns of standard size at an ever-accelerating pace, and the mechanics of the Northern cities were learning to handle them as though they had always done so. In the long view, that artillery was probably a decisive factor; even when the Army of the Potomac was defeated, the Confederates could never quite press home against it to obtain a complete result.

Prince George County, Maryland, the one touching the southern edge of the District of Columbia, was the eastern central of Confederate espionage. It was predominantly Southern in sympathy and comparatively thinly settled, with a particularly intricate system of roads among the trees. The Potomac was not too wide to be crossed in a small boat in this area, and there were many inlets where boats could be hidden. Moreover the Confederates had erected batteries on their side of the bank to annoy Potomac traffic (one of the causes for annoyance with McClellan was that he did not drive these batteries away), so that it was easy for spy couriers to reach rebel headquarters with the latest batch of information.

It was by this route that the famous Rose Greenhow sent her messages, including even reports of Cabinet meetings. But a thing as good as this cannot last forever. When Allen Pinkerton took up the business of espionage for the Union, he abandoned his detective work in the North, and into his place stepped that formidable character, Lafayette Baker, War Department detective, or as we should put it today, counterespionage agent.

Searching for arms in a Rebel's house in southern Maryland

Port Royal Harbor, South Carolina, Fort Walker interior

Mr. Baker was an expert at interrogation; when he located a suspicious character, he would have him in and soon reduce him to such a state of confusion that admissions were forthcoming. These admissions led to many houses in Prince George County, and upon these houses there presently descended the boys in blue.

It was not always arms they searched for, but the couriers themselves and the packets of dispatches that were usually carried in a standard format. Confederate espionage was efficiently, if slowly, brought under control and by 1863 was yielding only poor results.

The success at Hatteras opened the way for a far more important expedition against Port Royal, on an island off the South Carolina coast. Here there were two forts; Fort Walker on Hilton Head to the south, Fort Beauregard at the northern side of the entrance, each of them heavier works and mounting more guns than both the forts at Hatteras put together.

Walker was faced with masonry and had good elevation.

Against this complex Flag Officer S. F. DuPont brought four of the new 90-day gunboats (so-called because it took only that long to build them), six armed steamers, a side-wheel frigate, a sailing sloop, and one of the big screw frigates, with a corps of troops. The fleet arrived off the place on November 7; on the ninth DuPont started his bombardment, taking his line of ships in and moving with them in a long oval to fire first at one fort and then the other.

The ships fired altogether too fast; at the third round of the oval the rebels abandoned their guns, and when the troops went ashore, they found only the dead.

The effects of our fire were to be seen on every hand in the work. On the line along the front, three guns were dismounted by the enfilading fire of our ships. One carriage had been struck by a large shell and shivered to pieces, dismounting the heavy gun mounted upon it, and sending the

27

THE ERICSSON STEEL-CLAD BATTERY, NOW BUILDING AT GREEN POINT, LONG ISLAND.

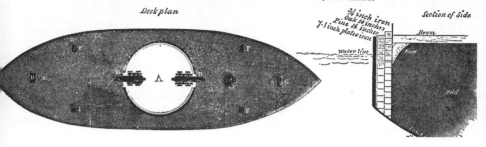

A: revolving battery.  B: 12-inch shell guns.  C: smoke stack.  D: propeller scuttle.  E: steering wheel.  F: hatchways.  G: forecastle hatch

splinters flying in every direction with terrific force. Between the guns and the foot of the parapet was a large pool of blood. Another carriage on the right was broken to pieces, and the guns on the water fronts were rendered useless by the enfilading fire from the gunboats on the left flank. All the houses and many of the tents about the work were perforated and torn by flying shell, and hardly a light of glass could be found intact in any building. No wonder then, that the rebels beat a hasty retreat.

At Port Royal there was demonstrated something beside the fact that ships could be assembled in sufficient number to overwhelm a fort; there was also demonstrated the fact that the fort might become ineffective against ships in motion, as DuPont kept his. Hatteras and Port Royal together may be said to have insured the success of the blockade along the Atlantic coast. The former opened the way into the North Carolina sounds; the latter provided a forward base, with a harbor which was secure in any weather, close to the area of operation.

Consequently, it became the major establishment of its kind, and all blockade and expeditionary work for the remainder of the war was carried out from it.

The building of *Monitor* was no secret from anyone, but to judge from the drawings, contemporaries had only the sketchiest idea of what the new ironclad would be like. *Harper's Weekly* reported on her thus:

The Ericsson battery, a sketch of which will be found on this page, is now in process of construction at the Continental Iron Works at Green Point, Long Island. She will be launched in the course of a few days. She is about 200 feet in length, with 36 foot beam and 11 feet depth of hold. Her hull is built of iron, and to protect her sides she is covered with a layer of oak 14 inches in thickness, another layer of pine 14 inches in thickness, the whole being plated with seven plates of one-inch iron, making her shot-proof. A revolving fort, which contains two 12-inch guns, is placed upon the deck near the centre. The diameter of the fort is 20 feet inside, and it is 10 feet in height. She will be propelled by a powerful Ericsson engine.

28

The description is not too bad, although the thickness of the armor is wrong. But the drawings! The artist had no idea of the armored deck and overhang, which were highly characteristic features; he placed the guns breech to breech, in a position where neither one of them could be loaded; he failed to give the ship a pilothouse, and if he is excusable for not realizing she had almost no freeboard at all, he is somewhat less so for conceiving of the "fort" as though it were built of courses of stone.

As early as Mill Spring, January 19, 1862, the Union began winning victories which were understood as victories but whose strategic importance remained unrecognized.

Full details have been received of the Battle of Somerset, Kentucky [said the weekly]. By the strategy of General Buell, Zollicoffer's army was surrounded by the divisions of Generals Thomas and Schoepff; perceiving which, Zollicoffer made a desperate attack upon the Union camp on Sunday morning. The battle began at four o'clock A.M. and lasted all day. General Zollicoffer was killed and his body found in a wagon. The rebels retreated and were followed to their intrenchments, which they abandoned during the night. The Southern papers profess to doubt the news of the affair.

There is more of the account, but this is the main line, and it is not very good reporting. Buell had nothing to do with it, and Schoepf was not a general. The battle lasted a good deal less than all day. But the most striking feature is that no one at the time seemed to realize that it marked a major break in the Confederate line of defense in the Middle West. Perhaps it was too early in the game for strategic realizations.

Abraham Lincoln was one of the people who quite justifiably felt that

The picket of the 10th Indiana Regiment discovering the approach of the Rebels at Mill Spring, Kentucky.

Why the Army of the Potomac doesn't move.

General view of Fort Donelson

McClellan should do something beside drill and hold reviews, and in January he ordered a move by February 22. On that same day *Harper's Weekly* issued an apology with pictures:

Whatever opportunities the fine weather of last month afforded for a forward movement, it is evidently out of the question to stir now, even if it accorded with General M'Clellan's strategy to do so. The Army of the Potomac is literally stuck in the mud, and no one attempts locomotion unless obliged.

But even as this was being printed, a general to whom mud mattered less than doing what he was there for was striking a truly decisive blow. On February 4, General U. S. Grant moved up the Tennessee and began landing troops from transports just below the Confederate stronghold of Fort Henry. Two days later a squadron of gunboats—Eads' gunboats; he got to build them after all—began shelling the place. By the time Grant arrived with his troops through bad and swampy ground, the place had surrendered.

He set out at once for the much more important Fort Donelson on the Cumberland, where there was a Con-federate army of considerable size, and was opposite the place on the fourteenth. Meanwhile the gunboats went around by the river to a position where the fort looked very much as it does in the picture shown here. They took a beating; their guns could not reach the uppermost batteries and the heavy plunging shot came right through their armor. Three of them were disabled and all driven out of action.

But Grant was now all around Donelson, and when the Confederates tried a sortie, barely repulsed, he launched a counterattack. It broke into the lines of the rebel works so seriously that it was evident they could not be held, and General S. B. Buckner, commanding, sent a note under a flag of truce to ask what terms Grant would offer for the surrender of the place.

It was then that Grant wrote the famous line that delighted a nation: *"No terms, except unconditional and immediate surrender can be accepted."*

He got his surrender, of course, and the Confederacy had not only lost a position of major strategic significance, but what was quite as important in the long run, a whole army. Man-

Major General Ulysses S. Grant, U.S.A., the hero of Fort Donelson

power shortage was one of the major causes of the downfall of the Confederacy.

On the whole the contemporary press did a very creditable job of reporting. *Harper's Weekly* picked up eyewitness accounts from correspondents at headquarters, with the 2nd Iowa and with one of the batteries of artillery, and the paper itself had an artist aboard the gunboat *Louisville*. All reported clearly and with what history has come to regard as accuracy, and if the strategic importance of the position was missed, as it usually was early in the war, the capture of the army was fully appreciated.

Perhaps too fully: the weekly gave it an editorial headed "The Beginning of the End" and saying: "Unless some unforseen accident occurs the whole Mississippi will be ours, from the Gulf to Cairo, by the 15th March." This

The surrender of Fort Donelson, February 16, 1862

Rebel prisoners at Camp Douglas, Chicago, Illinois

piece of early chicken-counting mentioned the forces operating under Burnside in North Carolina, under Buell, Halleck, and T. W. Sherman, but rather significantly failed to mention the still-immobile McClellan.

The portraits given to the country of its new national figure differ rather strikingly from what we would recognize today as a picture of U. S. Grant. Whatever the paper, they were all essentially the same, and labeled "from a photograph." One can only wonder where and when that photograph, which has not come to light, was made. The probability is that it was taken before the war — he seems a younger man — and that in copying it, the artist dressed him up in uniform.

No preparations had been made for handling prisoners, and the bulk of those from Donelson went to Chicago, where a *Harper's Weekly* man drew and described them:

A more woebegone appearing set of men it would be difficult for the reader to imagine. Compared with the laborers we are in the habit of seeing upon our public roads, they would suffer somewhat, being less hardy and healthy in build and complexion. It may have been from exposure and low diet, but they were all sallow faced, sunken eyed and apparently famishing. The uniforms of the Confederate prisoners are just no uniforms at all, being wholly ununified in color, cut, fashion, and manufacture. The majority stood gazing about the place, perfectly willing to be conversed with, and as willing to answer all questions."

In the minds of contemporaries there was never the slightest question about the importance of the events in Hampton Roads on March 8, and 9, 1862. *Harper's Weekly* took the strictly unusual step of devoting its whole central spread to the two battles in which *Virginia* (ex-*Merrimack*, with a *k* and not the way she was spelled

*Above:* The Rebel steamer *Merrimac* running down the frigate *Cumberland*

*Below:* The Ericsson battery *Monitor* driving off the *Merrimac*

35

by most of the press) sank two wooden frigates and was herself driven back by the "Ericsson battery" *Monitor*. The coverage, both in words and pictures was reasonably good, if one allows discount for the fact that the artist had to bring his ships too close together in order to show what they looked like. Rather strangely, the weekly, which liked to editoralize on almost everything connected with the war, had no comment at all on the two battles; perhaps it was felt that they spoke for themselves.

In the west, as in the east, both sides were still learning how to fight a war at this date; but the western armies were learning it rather the more rapidly, for they contained a higher proportion of farmers and backwoodsmen who knew something about living in the open. The camp scene in the corner of the picture is highly typical. Cooking was almost invariably done in iron pots, and the standard dish was stew, made of whatever meat and vegetables were available and served with hardtack. The bridge and the country are also a good sample of what existed at the time.

The Battle of Pea Ridge has been less reported than almost any other major engagement of the Civil War, whether by contemporaries or subsequent historians. It is hard to fit into any coherent story of the war; it took place in northern Arkansas, a theater ill-reported or not reported at all; it was neither preceded nor followed by any events of major importance. It was a loose, scrambling three-day action whose events are difficult to sort out. General S. R. Curtis, who won it, never did anything else of importance.

*Harper's Weekly* was reduced to printing an excerpt from his official report, and this more than three weeks after the event. General Franz Sigel, who gained a considerable and not

Grant's reconnaissance toward Columbus

The Battle of Pea Ridge, Arkansas. The final advance of our troops,
March 8, 1862

very well - deserved reputation, is barely mentioned in the dispatch; his reputation was the product of later word-of-mouth promotion, principally among the Germans, who were particularly strong in Missouri.

Yet if it is not literally true that the Confederate refugees from Pea Ridge populated the entire state of Montana, as was said later, the battle itself was of more importance than contemporaries realized. It did not end the war in the trans-Mississippi area, but it did break up the Confederate concentration there, deprived them of any hope of renewing the offensive into Missouri (compare Tennessee, where they were still fighting battles in December, 1864), and led directly to the conquest of Arkansas. General Van Dorn, one of the three Confederate commanders, was withdrawn to the east bank of the Mississippi, and the remainder of the Confederate force that had been assembled practically broke up into separate elements. Few battles of such permanent effect have gone so unrecognized.

It is the more surprising, then, to see *Harper's Weekly* giving it such good pictorial coverage. The Union troops advancing with their bayonets in the foreground are the usual conventionalized group; probably no troops in the war ever did advance in those precise lines, and almost certainly they never advanced shoulder to shoulder in the manner of these. But the broken, hilly country with patches of wood has been captured exactly, and it is possible to locate on a map of the battle just where this happened. That is, the picture bears every mark of being an eyewitness affair; but who the artist was who signs himself "M.N." remains a mystery. He was not one of the regular staff artists.

In March, 1862, the Army of the Potomac at last made the long-awaited forward movement. It moved in response to a scouting report that the

## Manassas Junction

Confederates were evacuating Manassas, and when it reached that celebrated junction found that the report was perfectly true. The weekly heralded it with:

Advance of the Grand Army of the Potomac, under General M'Clellan, into the rebel state of Virginia. About noon Generals M'Clellan and M'Dowell with their staffs, and two thousand cavalry for an escort, came up and took the road to Manassas. All along the left of the road was one continuous string of huts, tents, and forts, all empty now—not a human being or an animal showed themselves—not a sound save the clatter of the horses' hoofs, the shrill tones of the bugles, or the loud orders of the officers.

The Plains of Manassas are really what their name implies. The time was when there were objects that obstructed the range of vision, but they are all gone now; for miles around we have an unbroken view. On the track stood the wreck of a locomotive, and not far down the remains of four freight cars which had been burned; to the right, five hundred barrels of flour had been stove in, and two hundred barrels of vinegar and molasses had been allowed to try experiments in chemical combinations. Some fifty barrels of pork and beef had been scattered around in the mud, and a few hundred yards down the track a dense cloud of smoke was arising from the remains of a factory, which had been used for rendering up tallow and boiling bones. About a thousand good hides were stretched in a field close by upon stakes, and remain uninjured.

All the correspondents concur in saying that it was desolation intensified. Every thing the rebels could not carry away they destroyed, burning houses, clothes, and stores of all kinds, and rendering the place a perfect wilderness. We illustrate the intersection of the Orange and Alexandria Railroad with the Manassas Gap line. This is the "junction" which has given its name to the spot, and which imparted to the place so much military importance. The possession of the Junction gives us command of both roads.

It appears that every thing which the rebels could not destroy in their retreat was consumed. The store-houses at Manassas, with a large quantity of flour, were burned, and the Warrenton Station, together with the hotel and five or six dwellings. A freight train of fifty-two cars, loaded with commissary stores worth $20,000, was set on fire at Thoroughfare Station, twelve miles from Manassas, on the road to Winchester, but were rescued from destruction by our troops.

McClellan (it is now obvious) had gained a phantom victory. The Confederates abandoned not a thing they could not afford to abandon, and lost not a man. There was no follow-up; it was not in the Union general's plans that there should be, he was already committed to the water-borne expedition to the Peninsula. But what impresses one about contemporary accounts is the sense of outrage and injustice over the destructions of war, which none of the correspondents had seen before, and which were to become so prominent later without receiving any comment.

Island No. 10 is ours! It couldn't stand Commodore Foote's mortar shelling, and seems to have surrendered after one day's fighting, abandoning to us quantities of guns, stores, ammunition, etc., which the rebels cannot replace. How the garrison escaped, if they did escape, remains to be ascertained. Thus falls the second rebel strong-hold on the Mississippi.

Thus *Harper's* in accents of pardonable exultation, although the date was already beyond that March 15, when it had expected to see the whole river cleared. Actually, there were few actions of the war less understood at the time, or where the misunderstanding had more important effects.

Island No. 10 lay at the foot of an S curve in the river. Below it there are narrow strips of high ground on both the Tennessee and Mississippi sides, backed by impassable swamps; the Confederates had fortified both the island and the Tennessee shore opposite. When Foote's flotilla and the army under General John Pope approached the place, the problem was one of getting the troops into position where they could attack or cut off the fort.

The first try was by means of a canal, cut through the woods with incredible labor to New Madrid, at the top of the curve where the Mississippi swings south again. Pope's transports steamed through, and he was now on the high ground on the Missouri side, but this did him little good because the Tennessee shore opposite was lined with field batteries which prevented his crossing. The mortars shelled the place steadily but did not seem to be getting far and, in fact, were not.

On the night of April 4 in a thunderstorm Captain Henry Walke volunteered to run past the batteries with his ironclad *Carondelet* — only techni-

Union mortar rafts firing at Island No. 10

Ships in the forest; the New Madrid canal

*Carondelet* runs the batteries

cally an ironclad, since she was designed for end-on fighting, and half
her surface had no armor at all. He
lashed a coal barge filled with coal and
hay on one side of the vessel to give
additional protection, and he made it
without damage. Later the ironclad
knocked out the field batteries, Pope's
men could cross, and the island surrendered with 7000 men.

If the spot reporting had been of
the best character, this would have
been difficult enough to explain; but
actually the spot reporting was very
poor. First the mortars received all
the credit, although actually their fire
was more harassing than effective.
Later advices brought General Pope's
name to the fore and he was the new
hero, as great a man as Grant, who
had also taken a fortress and its garrison. By a fine historical irony, he was
credited with a greater achievement
than Grant's. It was quite as easy to
see the strategic significance of Island
No. 10 as it had been difficult to realize that of Donelson. Moreover, the
news of Grant's victory had come as a
surprise; Island No. 10 was the culmi-
nation of a siege operation, in which
excitements had an opportunity to

build up. So when a victorious commander from the west was needed to
straighten things out in the east, the
choice fell on Pope for reasons that
were rather emotional than intellec-
tual. Walke and the ironclad *Carondelet* were not even mentioned in the
papers at the time, and it was only
some time later, when correspondents
came back with reminiscent stories of
what they had seen, that the ship and
her captain began to get credit.

This was the first appearance of
Parson Brownlow, later so notorious
as the organizer of the carpetbaggers
during the Reconstruction period, the
man who called Andrew Johnson "that
dead dog in the White House;" and
it helps to explain some of his bitterness.

He was arrested by the civil authorities
upon the charge of treason, based upon
certain editorials in the [Knoxville] *Whig*.
He was taken to the county jail, thronged
at that time with Unionists, imprisoned on
suspicion of having participated in the
bridge-burning in the early part of November, and confined in a moist, narrow,
poorly lighted and ventilated dungeon
with twenty-four others. There were
neither beds nor chairs provided, nor was

41

Parson W. G. Brownlow

there rooms for all to lie down at one time. The food was of the meanest character. It told soon severely on the health of the Parson, and after a month he was stricken down with typhoid fever.

He gave a touching narrative of his sufferings in prison, of his illness, and the care with which the guards placed over him were doubled when he was so sick he could not turn in bed without assistance.

Finally he was released and conducted to the Union lines. Brownlow's account of affairs in east Tennessee, where there was a good deal of Union sentiment, had much to do with Lincoln's constant anxiety to have one of the Union armies move into that area.

The terrific battle of Shiloh, which for the first time convinced both sides that they were involved in a long and desperate struggle, did not get good pictorial coverage. There were only the usual conventionalized pictures of lines of men charging through country partly covered with trees, bearing little resemblance to the thick woods and steep declivites where the fighting was actually done. The artists got in later and did their best by the local scene. The reporting was somewhat better:

A terrible battle has taken place in the Southwest. A dispatch dated Pittsburg, *via* Fort Henry, April 9, says:

One of the greatest and bloodiest battles of modern days has just closed, resulting in the complete rout of the enemy, who attacked us at daybreak Sunday morning.

The battle lasted without intermission during the entire day and was again renewed Monday morning, and continued undecided until four o'clock in the afternoon, when the enemy commenced their retreat, and are still flying toward Corinth, pursued by a large force of our cavalry.

The slaughter on both sides is immense. We have lost in killed and wounded and missing from eighteen to twenty-four thousand; that of the enemy is estimated at from thirty-five to forty thousand.

On Sunday the advantage seems to have been undetermined; but on that evening General Buell arrived with fresh troops, and attacked the enemy at daybreak on Monday the 7th. Among the killed on the rebel side was their General-in-Chief, Albert Sidney Johnston, who was struck by a cannon-ball.

Except for the exaggeration of the enemy's losses, the usual thing in all wars and everywhere, this is a reasonably good account.

There must have been a certain piquant contrast for readers in the fact that the Army of the Potomac was reported as being at last on the move — up the Peninsula between the York and James rivers. That there was singularly little news of fighting from this front did not, as yet, make an impression. The public knew that the Confederates had some fortifications at Yorktown, and that McClellan was going to do something about them. For the rest Artist Waud described his own picture:

PITTSBURGH LANDING.

SHILOAH MEETING HOUSE.

General Buell's army crossing Duck River, at Columbia, Tennessee, to reinforce General Grant

Baxters Zouaves making a road through the woods in front of Yorktown

Rebels outside their works at Yorktown, reconnoitering with dark lanterns

"The country about Yorktown is a swamp covered with pines, little clearing being made here and there for farms. No roads exist of any account for military operations, therefore our soldiers have had to make them."

The most interesting thing about the picture of a rebel picket is that it represents the earliest appearance on page one of "our staff artist, Winslow Homer." He stayed with *Harper's Weekly* throughout the war, and his handling was always brilliant, even though he had to depend upon imagination for some details. It is doubtful, for example, whether many Southern regiments wore the *kepi* which was practically a badge in the Union service; and it is somewhat unlikely that a group on picket duty would go out with fixed bayonets. The dark lanterns are less open to question; they were probably there.

*Harper's Weekly* had an artist with Farragut at New Orleans, but he did a poor job with his pencil, and the pictures are from the rival publication, *Leslie's*. The unnamed *Harper's* artist did turn in copy, however:

On the 24th Commodore Farragut determined to run past the forts. The fleet was formed in three divisions, and proceeded to steam up the river.

At precisely twenty minutes of four o'clock the enemy opened fire from Fort St. Philip. At that moment I hoisted our largest Star-Spangled Banner to the peak, and then hastening forward, decked the fore and main each with an emblem of power and justice. Full speed was given to the ship, the engineers did their duty nobly, and on we went, as it were, into the jaws of death. At five minutes of four o'clock our bow guns belched fire and smoke and a messenger in the shape of a nine-inch shell was sent to Fort Jackson. In a few minutes more the broadside firing was commenced. Both forts were replying as fast as they could. Broadside after broadside was delivered to them in rapid succession, while the mortar vessels were adding to the dreadful noise.

In the midst of this awful scene, down came a tremendous fire-raft, and the Ram shoved her under our port quarter. The flames caught our rigging and side, and for a moment it seemed we must fall a prey to the ravages of fire. The fire hose was on hand, and we soon subdued the flames and gave the Ram a dose of rifle shell. The river and banks were one sheet of flame, and the messengers of death were

Engagement with a Rebel ally

The battle at the forts: New Orleans: *Jackson, Cayuga,* ram, *Pensacola, Mississippi,* Rebel boat, Rebel boat, *Varuna, Oneida*

moving with lightning swiftness in all directions. Steadily we plied shell and grape, interspersed with shrapnel. Rebellion began to quake; her boats were fast being riddled by well-directed broadsides, and they who were able to made for the shore to run them on. Some were on fire, and others were sinking. Our boys were cheering with a hearty good-will, and well they might, for we were past the forts. Our ship had been on fire three times, and she was riddled from stem to stern. The cabin was completely gutted, the starboard steerage all torn up, and the armory all knocked into "pi."

Next morning the fleet arrived at New Orleans.

The view from our decks was one such as will never, in all probability, be witnessed again. The levee was crowded by an excited mob. The smoke of the ruins of millions worth of cotton and shipping at times half concealed the people. Men, women, and children were armed with pistols, knives and all manner of weapons. Some cheered for Jeff Davis, Beauregard, etc., and used the most vile and obscene language toward us and the good old flag.

The fall of New Orleans, largest city and greatest port of the South, made a considerable contemporary impression. Before it took place, the editorials were all about the prospects of Franco-British intervention. That they stopped abruptly is an indication of the abrupt change in mental climate.

It will be remembered that after the Battle of Shiloh, General Henry W. Halleck, who had overall direction of the Union armies in the west, came down to Pittsburg Landing, took command of the combined armies of Grant and Buell, called in Pope's force from the Mississippi, and began a campaign against Corinth, Mississippi. He prided himself on being a scientific soldier, and began to apply methods designed for the narrower areas of Europe, fortifying every step of the way and building roads as he went. Corinth did have considerable strategic importance as a main junction point on the railroad Memphis-Chattanooga-Charleston, one of the two big lateral lines crossing the Confederacy, but almost as he reached it, Memphis fell to the river fleet, and the Confederate forces escaped from Corinth without serious harm.

It is important to understand the temper of the times in which these

Corduroying roads to Cornith

events took place. In the east McClellan was making the slowest of progress with his "siege" of Yorktown, a place which turned out to have been defended chiefly by wooden guns. After Shiloh, a feeling had grown up that, although Grant had won at Shiloh, he was somehow responsible for the immense loss of life in that battle; that he was a rather crude bungler. There was a general disposition to attribute the victory to Halleck's strategic combination, which had brought the armies of Grant and Buell together there.

To this feeling Halleck himself largely contributed. He complained to Washington that he could get no proper returns from Grant, that Grant was lax in his paper work, etc., etc., and made Grant his second in command, with no duties to speak of. Thus Grant, who had won two great victories in the west, practically disappeared for the time being. There were no longer pictures of him or copy about him; Halleck got all the press. And since he was not doing any fighting either, the two *Harper's* artists with his army, Mosler and Simplot, were busy with sketches of road building and rear areas, while the correspondents tell us:

The country around Corinth is of a rolling timbered land, sweeping in successive ridges and flat boggy hollows for miles in every direction. These latter make it a matter of difficulty to approach the place with artillery. The rebels have embraced a circuit of hills several miles in which they are encamped. The length of these works is estimated at nine miles, and they are re-

48

Hamburg Landing, Tennessee, commissary depot of Major General Halleck's army

Naval battle off Memphis

ported to have several heavy siege pieces in position at the salient points. There is first an abbatis of felled timber a mile from the guns, which, while it will present an obstacle to the passage of our lines, will present an admirable cover for our sharpshooters. Beyond the timber is a rifle-trench, at a few hundred yards distance from the guns. Behind this breast-work it is thought the enemy's forces will be lodged after the place is invested. The inner line is a series of angles and bastions running from hill-top to hill-top, a heavy gun being placed to cover every approach.

That we may be prepared for any untoward occurrence as a stampede, a reverse, or an attempt on the part of the rebels to pierce our lines, our men have been engaged busily yesterday and to-day in erecting a strong line of breast-works formed of timber and branches covered with dirt, which are again masked so as to conceal them from the view of the enemy. The most commanding positions have been seized, the first line about eight miles from Corinth. With a cleared space in front and guns placed in commanding positions the enemy can not approach our line without being subjected to a murderous fire.

But a few days since the mud was the greatest impediment to our progress. We are now at the other extreme. So far from being troubled with too much moisture, we have not enough to drink, much less for other purposes. Our men are digging for water, and the result is a thick whitish mixture of nauseous taste is all that can be had potable. Horses are ridden a mile to a muddy, stagnant pool, and not infrequently the soldiers are reduced to the same extremity. Lemons and liquors are in great demand to render the water palatable.

In other words, Halleck was thinking in terms of a siege, or at least letting the correspondents think that was what he was thinking about. It is probable that he was quite surprised when Beauregard did not stay in Corinth to be besieged.

Today it is often difficult to realize how much the Civil War armies depended upon water transportation, especially for supplies, and how greatly the Union gained by its early naval victories on the Mississippi and its vast system of tributaries. No campaign in the west was really fought out of range from a river until Rosecrans moved toward Chattanooga in the summer of 1863, and he encountered enormous difficulty in keeping his supply up. The railroads were short, often had different gauges, and seldom bridged the big rivers.

The naval battle off Memphis was the only fleet action of the Civil War, and it was decisive. After the fall of Island No. 10, the defense of Memphis was left in the hands of a squadron of eight rams, converted from river steamers, with armor of pressed cotton bales and iron-shod prows.

Against them came Commodore C. H. Davis, with four of his ironclads. At the last moment there dashed through the Union line four wooden rams, built by Colonel C. H. Ellet, carrying no guns at all, but specially braced for ramming. In a brief action, all but one of the Confederate craft were sunk or driven ashore, and Memphis surrendered.

*Harper's Weekly* made the somewhat unjustified assumption that this was the end of Confederate defense on the river.

The possession of the river not only divides the rebel states, but it insures, in a given period of time, the surrender of the rebel armies in Virginia and Mississippi from famine. In the rebel realm as inclosed by the Mississippi River, there is no beef. Without beef the rebels can not fight. Pork and corn may answer for a while; but unless the rebel commissaries can renew their requisitions upon the pastures of Texas, Missouri, Kentucky and Tennessee, their armies will scatter.

An excellent example of the type of strategic wishful thinking which has by no means been limited to the Civil War.

Feeding the Negro children under charge of the military authorities at Hilton Head, South Carolina

At the posts seized by the Union along the Southern coast, the handling of contrabands became a daily increasing problem. Work was found for some of the men, although at least one commander complained that they were good for nothing but hoeing and he had no hoeing to do. The rest simply had to be fed. Some interest attaches to what is being dished out to them. The probability strongly favors hominy.

No matter how much coverage was given or not given to other theaters, the main preoccupation of the weekly press remained with the Army of the Potomac. It drew the best artists and correspondents and the space devoted to it exceeded that given to all the other armies put together. Quite an affair was made of the Battle of Williamsburg, for instance, the weeklies giving it more space than Shiloh.

*Harper's Weekly*, ever hopeful, referred to "the section of country where General M'Clellan is operating, and where the last act of the drama of Rebellion will be performed," and went on to comment on its pictures:

The rebel general had seen our weakness, and sent a force of four thousand infantry and a regiment of cavalry to attack us in the rear. As soon as they appeared in sight General Hancock ordered the artillery to retreat, and prepared to give them a proper reception.

Waiting till the enemy had approached within two hundred yards, he placed himself at the head of his column, and, taking off his cap, turned to his men and said to them, as only General Hancock can say it, "Gentlemen, charge!" and with a yell they rushed upon the enemy, scattering them in every direction.

*Above:* General Hancock's brigade charging the Rebels at the Battle of Williamsburg.
*Below:* General Hooker's division engaging the enemy at the Battle of Williamsburg

Our troops marching down into the trenches before Richmond

The Army of the Potomac. Our outlying picket in the woods

McClellan also thought very highly of his achievement at Williamsburg. The way he put it was:

As soon as I came upon the field the men cheered like fiends, and I saw at once that I could save the day. It would have been easy for me to have sacrificed 10,000 lives in taking Yorktown, and I presume the world would have thought it more brilliant. The Battle of Williamsburg was more bloody. Had I reached the field three hours earlier, I could have gained greater results, and have saved a thousand lives.

In another dispatch he added: "Hancock was superb."

Now this represents an early stage in the game of McClellan promoting McClellan, both by what he said directly and what he gave the press. What actually happened at Williamsburg was that the Confederates were fighting a rear-guard action after the Yorktown fake had been exposed; they were only anxious to get away to the lines around Richmond. Hancock arrived late on the field, and his charge produced no particular results; the divisions of Hooker and Kearny did most of what fighting there was.

McClellan himself arrived after everything was over and only rode along the lines while the troops cheered him, as they were usually willing to do. How he could have saved a thousand lives does not appear from the record; the returns after the battle showed only 450 killed. There is no sign in any contemporary account that the press realized what was going on; indeed probably no one then with the army could tell what was going on.

The artists, however, made excellent reports, and often accompanied them by observations:

The road and water approaches to Richmond are open to within twelve or fifteen miles of the city, and the enemy is in force

General McClellan's army on the march through the woods from Williamsburg toward Richmond

beyond these points. The state of the roads is such that it will require some days to get the army up to these points. Ever since last Monday, a week ago, the army has been moving from West Point to this place, a distance of only twenty miles. The nature of the soil is such that it is found necessary to construct military roads nearly the entire distance in order to transport the artillery and baggage-wagons. This work has been admirably performed by the engineer corps of General Daniel P. Woodbury.

The Battle of Mechanicsville was an inconsiderable skirmish during Joe Johnston's withdrawal to the lines he had built for the defense of Richmond, but the weeklies gave it a heavy play:

This morning at daybreak the rebels opened upon the little band that had driven them across the river at New Bridge. The cavalry and artillery were encamped across the river, and the infantry close by upon the opposite side, but in supporting distance. To our right was a

little village called Mechanicsville. In a grove this side a battery of four guns commenced to fire solid shot; before us was an open field, and the fire was at once returned, but no damage being done in half an hour, or the firing being unsatisfactory, Wheeler's battery of four pieces, and Davidson's brigade in the following order —Seventy-seventh New York, Colonel J. B. M'Keon; Thirty-third New York, Forty-ninth New York, Seventh Maine, Colonel Mason—were ordered to take the battery. They at once marched up half a mile, when the rebel infantry were seen drawn up in line of battle in front of the battery. Wheeler's battery at once halted and opened upon them, dealing out a terrific fire of canister and shell. It was returned with but little loss on our side. We could now see four squadrons of rebel cavalry and two regiments of gray coats.

After firing some time, the Seventy-seventh New York and Thirty-third New York advanced again, and, in marching up, received a hearty volley of musketry and solid shot from their 12-pounders, with a

The Army of the Potomac. The Rebels evacuating Mechanicsville under fire of Union batteries

Camp punishments. Drumming a coward out of the ranks

"charge bayonets," and one of the most terrific roars that seemed like the bursting of a huge cataract from its barriers, on they rushed; first the cavalry fled, and before the infantry got close enough to see the whites of their eyes, their infantry broke and ran in all directions through the woods. Down went knapsacks, canteens and muskets. The infantry pursued them cautiously, and found one wounded man upon the field who belonged to a Georgia regiment. Their killed and wounded were taken away with them with this exception.

Now it is obvious that if there had been such a panic as described, either the Confederates could hardly have carried away their killed and wounded with them, or that there were not many killed and wounded. But the account does contain between the lines a fact not usually appreciated about the Civil War. Those thrilling bayonet charges, so often described, seldom reached their goal; in point of fact either one side stopped charging or the other went away.

This can be referred to the overwhelming influence of convention. Just as the artists invariably pictured a charge as a line of men advancing shoulder to shoulder and in perfect step across ground that was nearly always accidented and frequently spotted with trees or brush, so the reporters nearly always spoke of the same thing. The reality was quite different. "Did you ever charge shoulder to shoulder?" a veteran of the war was asked. "No," was his reply; "God don't make men who could stand that."

Yet the public continued to believe the convention rather than the reality, and there are not a few soldier diaries from the Civil War which express surprise over the discovery that it wasn't true after all; that you advanced in a ragged line, taking advantage of every feature of the landscape and often pausing to fire.

The problem of punishments has vexed every army since Alexander

The surgeon at work at the rear during an engagement

the Great. If you put a man in the guardhouse, you must put another one at the door of it to watch him, and in the field there are no guard-houses anyway. If you court-martial him, three or five officers must be taken from their proper business to handle the matter, and evidence has to be submitted. Most commanders in the Civil War tried to make their punishments ingenious, but not a waste of time to perform.

*Harper's Weekly* comments on its picture of a field surgeon at work:

Away to the rear, under the green flag, which is always respected among civilized soldiers, the surgeon and his assistants receive the poor wounded soldiers, and swiftly minister to their needs. Arteries are tied, ligatures and tourniquets applied, flesh wounds hastily dressed, broken limbs set, and sometimes, when haste is essential, amputations performed within sight and sound of the cannon. Of all officers the surgeon is often the one who requires most nerve and most courage. Upon his coolness and judgment depend the lives of a large proportion of the wounded.

But George Alfred Townsend, the famous war correspondent, paints a somewhat difficult and more personal picture:

I rode across the fields to the Hogan, Curtis and Gaines mansions, for some of the wounded had been deposited in each of them. All the cow-houses, wagon-sheds, hay-barracks, hen-coops, Negro cabins and barns were turned into hospitals. The floors were littered with "corn-shucks" and fodder, and the maimed, gashed, and dying lay confusedly together. A few, slightly wounded, stood at windows, relating incidents of the battle, but at the doors sentries stood with crossed bayonets, to keep out idlers and gossips. The mention of my vocation was an "open sesame," and I went unrestrained, into all the largest hospitals. In the first of them an amputation was being performed, and at the door lay a little heap of human fingers, feet, legs, and arms. I shall not soon forget the bare-armed surgeons, with bloody instruments, that leaned over the rigid and insensible figure, while the comrades of the subject looked horrifiedly at the scene.

The grating of the murderous saw drove me into the open air, but in the second hospital which I visited, a wounded man had just expired, and I encountered his body at the threshold. Within, a sickening smell of mortality was almost insupportable, but by degrees I became accustomed

Battle at St. Charles, White River, Arkansas. Explosion of the *Mound City*

to it. The lanterns hanging around the room streamed fitfully upon the red eyes, the half-naked figures. All were looking up, and saying, in pleading monotone: "Is that you, doctor?" Men with their arms in slings went restlessly up and down, smarting with fever. Those who were wounded in the lower extremities, body, or head, lay upon their backs, tossing even in sleep. They listened peevishly to the wind whistling through the chinks of the barn. They followed one with rolling eyes. Soldiers sat by the severely wounded, laving their sores with water. In many wounds the ball still remained, and the discolored flesh was swollen unnaturally. There were some who had been shot in the bowels, and now and then they were frightfully convulsed, breaking into shrieks and shouts. The act of calling seemed to dull the pain. Many were unconscious and lethargic, moving their fingers and lips mechanically, but never more to open their eyes upon the light; they were already going through the valley and the shadow.

This is candid and, of somewhat adjectival, perfectly clear reporting. The point about it that will strike anyone who had anything to do with reporting the late war is that the censors would probably jump down the throat of anyone who attempted to report that way today, accusing him of making pacifist propaganda. The Civil War had more reverence for facts when it could get them.

In June, 1862, General Curtis started an offensive into Arkansas and asked that gunboats come up the White River to support him. Two of the ironclads, *Mound City* and *St. Louis,* were sent, with the old Rodgers timber-clad *Conestoga.* At St. Charles they found a Confederate steamer sunk across the river with a battery on the bluff above. Commander A. H. Kilty made the mistake of engaging it without waiting for the troops who had been landed just below. A shot came through one of his portholes, ranged the length of the deck, and tore out the whole steam system of *Mound City.* There was an explosion of steam so frightful that next morning only 25 of his crew of 175 answered roll call.

The interesting point is that once more no attempt was made to cover up or excuse. Both in the text and the illustration the weekly told the story fairly and fully, setting it down as a defeat. But there were no field censors during the Civil War, and the censors on the telegraph lines seldom interfered, except with dispatches passing through Washington.

On May 30, Joe Johnston attacked McClellan's army at Fair Oaks, with the intention of driving it away from Richmond. Considering the number and quality of the correspondents and

The Army of the Potomac. Burying the dead and burning dead horses at Fair Oaks Station, Virginia

artists with the Army of the Potomac, the battle received surprisingly poor coverage. *Harper's Weekly* printed nothing at the time but McClellan's dispatch and the usual highly imaginative picture of a bayonet charge. Only later did it get around to the aftermath of the battle, burying the dead and burning dead horses. Yet it was the most serious fighting in which the Army of the Potomac had yet engaged, and the Union casualties were 5031, more than in all the rest of the campaign up to this time.

The reasons for this lack of interest are rather complex. After Shiloh, casualty figures in themselves had lost the power to impress. There had been a battle and many were killed; that was all there was to it. Nor was Fair Oaks impressive on the map. Nobody gained or lost any visible amount of geography. The battle was also one of those confused, difficult affairs like Pea Ridge, fought between green troops, in which there were only incidents, no central line of movement. Yet it is impossible to avoid the impression that the neglect was at least partly due to the influence of the growing McClellan claque.

For Fair Oaks was the battle in which Joe Johnston was wounded, to be replaced by Lee, and almost immediately thereafter Lee opened the campaign in which he called Jackson from the Shenandoah and drove McClellan from his position before Richmond to Harrison's Landing on the James, a position without a future. The reporting in this case was neither full nor fair, whether by fault of the correspondents, the editors, or (most likely) McClellan himself. Not that he censored things; he had established good relations with the correspondents, they did not want to let him down, and the information he gave out was probably quite as mendacious as his own dispatches for the period.

The opening of the campaign was announced as: "A Skirmish Before Richmond."

On 25th June, our pickets on the left were advanced considerably, under sharp resistance on the part of the enemy. At 3½ o'clock General M'Clellan telegraphed that the picket lines of General Kearney and one half of General Hooker were where he desired them to be, and that he hoped soon to accomplish all he aimed at for the day. A 5 o'clock he telegraphed that the affair was over, and that he had gained his point fully. The enemy was driven out of his camps in front, and all was quiet. While this important movement was being made on the left General Fitz-John Porter, farther to the right, succeeded in silencing the enemy's batteries in his front.

When the show was over, this was the comment:

After one of the most exciting weeks of the war, we can at last thank God that the Army of the Potomac is safe, and is really nearer the accomplishment of the work that it has been appointed to do than it has ever been. That General M'Clellan was placed in a position of danger by the sudden appearance of Jackson's army on his right flank, and that in the six battles which occurred on 26th, 27th, 28th, 29th, and 30th June, and 1st July, we lost a large number of gallant men and officers is true. But it is also true that the change of base from the Pamunkey to the James River had been determined, and actually begun, before Jackson made his appearance. It is also true that notwithstanding the furious attacks of enormous rebel armies, M'Clellan's forces moved toward the James River by the roads and at the rate directed by their commander; and after five days' terrible fighting, reached the point he had selected for them ten days previously. Lastly, it is also true that, while we may have lost from 15,000 to 18,000 men in killed, wounded and missing, we have gained the support of the James River gun-boat flotilla, which is worth an army of 100,000 men.

On the other hand, the rebels, who according to the papers, are returning thanks

Fighting in the woods during the seven days

for a victory, have suffered so terribly that prisoners estimate their losses at 40,000 men. They have gained possession of the swamps where we have lost so many men by fever—nothing more.

On the whole, then, we have gained more than we have lost, and the rebels have lost more than they have gained, by the series of battles ending on 1st July. And now, if M'Clellan is promptly reinforced, we shall soon see how absurd and wretched it was to talk of M'Clellan's movement as a retreat.

This was editorial, to be sure, but the accompanying news dispatches do no more than list the battles and repeat the claims of enormous Confederate losses. The noteworthy point about this apology, which might have been written by McClellan himself, is that it includes the phrases "enormous rebel armies" and "if M'Clellan is promptly reinforced." These were precisely the two claims on which the general's whole campaign had been based—not the military campaign but the political and publicity one. Ever since he reached the Peninsula, he had been bombarding Washington with statements of the prodigious enemy numbers, accompanied by requests for more troops, down to the day when he telegraphed Lincoln: "You have done your best to sacrifice this army," a portion of the dispatch rather fortunately deleted in the telegraph office before it reached the President.

McClellan's behavior, his vanity, his constant demands for more troops to deal with a Confederate army he already heavily outnumbered, are part of the ordinary historical record. The curious point is how the editors came to fall for his publicity and

California Joe, of the Berdan Sharpshooters

repeat his phrases. Certainly, some of them were no fools, as they demonstrated by their handling of other campaigns and other generals. Certainly, some of them must have had information that should have led to suspicion. Did all the correspondents miss the fact that one of McClellan's generals of division had said publicly: "I, Philip Kearney, an old soldier, enter my solemn protest against this order for retreat."?

It is hard to believe; and the key probably lies in Lincoln's own reaction, which sums up that of the civilian mind. When Senator Ben Wade came to him with a demand that McClellan be dispensed with, the President said: "Whom would you put in his place?"

"Anybody!"

"Wade, anybody will do for you, but I must have somebody."

That is, circumstance and the publicity machine had combined so effectively that as of the date of the Seven Days' Battles, there was no visible alternative to McClellan. Lincoln, characteristically, tried an outflanking maneuver. The same issues of the weeklies that told of McClellan's "change of base" also carried the news that General John Pope had been called from the west to head a new Army of Virginia. It was to be organized from the troops around Washington, some from the Shenandoah Valley, and a corps or two drawn from McClellan for a strike along the direct overland route through Manassas that McClellan had refused to take.

"California Joe," who seems never to have had another name, early became celebrated. Comment:

California Joe was first heard of by the public when the army was before Yorktown. I spent an hour yesterday in his tent. He is a character. I was surprised at his age. He is past fifty, but he looks a score of years younger. He stands as straight as an arrow, has an eye as keen as a hawk, nerves as steady as can be, and an endowment of hair and whiskers Reubens would have liked for a patriarchal portrait. He has spent years of his life shooting grizzly bears in the forests and fastnesses of California, and carries a telescopic rifle that in his hand will carry a long ways and with terrific accuracy. For several days past he has occupied as a shooting-place a hole dug in the ground just big enough for himself. His unerring rifle has made many a rebel bite the dust. He says he likes the sport, and he means to keep it up.

Farragut's fleet from the Gulf and Davis' gunboats from upstream met above Vicksburg. A great loop of the Mississippi makes a peninsula with a

Cutting the canal opposite Vicksburg

narrow neck opposite the town. Almost immediately there was laid on a project for cutting a canal through this peninsula, as one had been cut at Island No. 10, with the idea that transports could carry the army through it and reach the high ground on the east bank below the fortress.

It didn't work, for reasons here described:

When we arrived, it had been completed only through that portion of the neck which is inside the levee. It was about fifteen feet wide and three, or three and a half feet deep. This, it was supposed, was of sufficient depth to allow the water of the river to flow through, but when the levee at each end of it was cut through, it was found to be above the level of the water. The mountain would not come to Mohammed, and some wiseacre determined to make it come by placing an old stern-wheel boat at the lower side of the entrance to the canal, to work her wheel, and so paddle the water up into it, which succeeded in wetting the bottom of the canal just enough to make it muddy, but no more. This experiment in making water run uphill not proving very successful, it was determined to deepen the ditch. One half of the bottom was cut five feet deeper. By this means a small thread of water, about a foot wide, was decoyed into it, where it remains at present, looking very much bewildered.

The candor of this reporting is in rather striking contrast to the kindness the press showed McClellan, who

64

on the very same page was given credit for conceiving a plant for bisecting the Confederacy along the Mississippi, and again cutting it in half by an advance from Memphis to Charleston. The Mississippi line was, of course, obvious, but there is no evidence that the second plan existed anywhere except in editorial minds.

Meanwhile, the Confederates had secretly completed the ironclad ram *Arkansas* up the Yazoo River. On July 15 she ran through the combined fleets, exchanging blows. The upshot was that Farragut's fleet went back downstream, Davis' back up.

The boys were learning. Contemporary accounts of the misfortunate Second Bull Run campaign began with the expected note of cheerfulness, then rapidly became mendacious and obfuscating until it was no longer possible to conceal the fact of defeat —

a sufficiently curious study. The running account began with editorial matter on Pope's fine prospects, then:

The Army of Virginia has drawn blood. At Cedar Mountain on Saturday August 9, General Banks's corps — about 7000 strong — encountered some 15,000 of the enemy, under Jackson and Ewell, and fought them till nightfall. The battle did not lead to any substantial results that day. But on Sunday the rebels fell back toward the Rapidan, and sent in a flag of truce for permission to bury their dead. At the same time heavy reinforcements were pouring in from the other corps composing Pope's army, and Sigel was at the front. This may be deemed an auspicious commencement of the new campaign in Northern Virginia.

It should be remembered that Pope and Sigel bore high reputations at the time; all the same Cedar Mountain was a defeat, and the correspondents were covering up. Next:

The Rebel ram *Arkansas* running through the Union fleet off Vicksburg

General Pope has fallen back from Culpepper to the north bank of the Rappahannock, followed by the enemy in great force. From Wednesday, 20th, up to Saturday, 23d, there had been almost constant fighting all along the Rappahannock. On Wednesday there was only a single skirmish, the rebels driving back our pickets, but retiring before a cavalry charge. On Thursday five rebel regiments had a contest with Sigel's advance, and suffered pretty severely. On Friday they got to work in earnest, and the fight raged hotly all day along the river, the enemy trying to cross. They did not succeed. On Saturday an artillery duel began at four o'clock and lasted all day, the enemy still working up along the river to turn our flank. The boldest dash of the enemy was that made by Stuart's cavalry upon Catlett's Station, where they succeeded in capturing General Pope's papers and money.

There is no hint here that anyone realized what the presence of Stuart (he was actually the cover for Jackson's corps) at Catlett's meant. Actually, it meant that the Confederates were across Pope's communications and he would have to go back in a hurry. A week later the story was:

The rebels have transferred the bulk of their army to the vicinity of Manassas Junction, and the bulk of our Eastern army is there to oppose them. At the hour we write we know that four battles have been fought with no decided success on either side. Our troops, outnumbered as they are, have, however, held their own. Manassas Junction and the Heights of Centreville are ours still. We have taken a large number of prisoners, and killed a great many rebels. Our enemy can probably say the same. Such is the situation at present. Possibly before these lines are read it may have changed materially.

This is pretty poor reporting, but the trouble is discernably in the lack of good front-line dispatches. Our troops were by no means holding their own; they were being badly beaten, but censorship was sitting on the telegraph wires Northward, probably hoping for a change in the complexion, and no really candid account stood a chance of getting through. It is perhaps indicative that the pictorial coverage of the Second Bull Run campaign was practically nil; while the text was giving this garbled account of the campaign, the illustrations were a portrait of General Pope, a panorama of a training camp in Pennsylvania, pictures of the new ironclads, a scene in southwestern Tennessee and "A Gallant Color-Bearer."

66

Spring on the Rappahannock

The last resting place

R.R. Bridge over the Chickahominy

Rail Road into Richmond

Bridge-builders.

The Rebel army crossing the fords of the Potomac for the invasion of Maryland

Another week, and the apologies began:

The leading events of the week which has elapsed since we last wrote have been the retreat of the national forces to Washington, after a series of battles, and the invasion of Maryland by the rebels. These transactions have filled the public mind with chagrin, and loud complaints against the administration and the generals in the field have appeared in leading journals. Presses not suspected of lukewarmness in the cause have not scrupled to declare that the campaign has thus far been productive of nothing but disgrace to the national arms, and that unless some radical change—either in the cabinet, or in the military leaders, or in the general policy of the war—be instantly effected, we may as well succumb at once. It is quite likely that the practical effect of this sort of writing may be beneficial.

...with considerably more in the same tone of voice, and for once, some emphasis on the western theater, where things were going better. But the really big news was not that the rebels had invaded the North for the first time but that McClellan was back in command. It is thoroughly characteristic that the weekly should announce it with a front-page picture of him riding through the streets of Frederick, being applauded and pelted with roses.

From what we now know, it is clear that the Confederates really expected to find Maryland at least sympathetic enough to making the obtaining of supplies easy, and probably expected no inconsiderable number of recruits to join them. Contemporary accounts are quite agreed that the reality they found is accurately indicated by the cartoon above. The rebels were valiant and well led; but Maryland found them a band of ragamuffins and was disinclined to join fortunes with a declining concern.

But by this date the threads were already drawing toward Antietam, the only battle McClellan fought in which he was not attacked, and the heaviest yet engaged in the east. It was a product of Harper's Ferry, the gate of the railroad lines westward from Washington, where there had been an arsenal until it was burned out on Virginia's secession. Contemporaries had a lively sense of its strategic importance; of the fact that the lines of communication northeast out of the Shenandoah and those from Washington crossed there. Lee was one of those contemporaries; he detached Jackson with nearly half his army to take the place and its garrison. In all the histories one can find the story of how his orders to Jackson were found by an Indiana private, wrapped around a cigar; of how McClellan found in them an elixir of lost youth, and moved to get between the parts of the Confederate Army, but moved so slowly that they were united before he attacked at Antietam Creek.

The battle received an extremely good press and, what is more, an accurate press except for McClellan's part. Hooker was praised, Doubleday was praised, and especially Burnside. The operative passage in the contemporary report runs like this, headlined "M'Clellan to the Rescue":

M'Clellan remounts his horse, and with Porter and a dozen officers of his staff rides away to the left in Burnside's direction. Sykes meets them on the road — a good soldier, whose opinion is worth taking. The three Generals talk briefly together. It is easy to see that the moment has come when every thing may turn on one order given or withheld, when the history of the battle is only to be written in the thoughts and purposes and words of the General.

Burnside's messenger rides up. His message is, "I want troops and guns. If you do not send them I can not hold my posi-

General McClellan entering the town of Frederick, Maryland.
The popular welcome

The Battle of Antietam, fought

tion for half an hour." M'Clellan's only answer for the moment is a glance at the western sky. Then he turns and speaks very slowly: "Tell General Burnside that this is the battle of the war. He must hold his ground till dark at any cost. I will send him Miller's battery. I can do nothing more. I have no infantry." Then, as the messenger was riding away, he called him back, "Tell him if he can *not* hold his ground, then the bridge, to the last man!—always the bridge! If the bridge is lost, all is lost."

The sun is already down; not a half hour of daylight is left. Till Burnside's messenger came it seemed plain to every one that the battle could not be finished to-day. None suspected how near was the peril of defeat, of sudden attack on exhausted forces—how vital to the safety of the army and the nation were those fifteen thousand waiting troops of Fitz John Porter in the hollow. But the rebels halted instead of pushing on; their vindictive cannonade died away as twilight faded.

Concealed in this account there are several important facts. McClellan obviously was not rescuing anything by telling Burnside he must hold the position he had gained. But more im-

portantly, he was not defending against Confederate attacks, he was attacking with superior forces, and he was holding Porter's 15,000 men out of the attack when they might easily have tipped the balance and converted a dubious victory into a crushing one.

That is, McClellan was not thinking of what he might win, but of what he might lose; and the McClellan claque, promoted by the general himself, was quite ready to accept his version and pass it on to the readers.

The handling of wounded in the Civil War was always a ghastly business, but it became notably better in the Union service after Second Bull Run, owing chiefly to the Sanitary Commission, a kind of volunteer Red Cross, which not only jacked the government up about hospitals and the food in them, but also provided the soldiers with things like tracts and underwear. During the first year of the war the Surgeon-General, a superannuated old party named Dr. Clement A. Finley, chiefly noted for his hostility to female nurses, ham-

September 17, 1862. Burnside holding the hill

General view of Harper's Ferry and the Maryland Heights

The Battle of Antietam. Carrying off the wounded after the battle

pered the Sanitary Commission as much as he could, but he got into a row with Stanton and was ejected.

The Sanitary Commission secured the appointment of Dr. William A. Hammond. The first thing he wanted was an ambulance service. The generals objected on the ground that it was unmilitary; the quartermaster corps had always handled ambulances and should continue to do so. This stuck until Second Bull Run, when the reports of heavy casualties caused a call for volunteer nurses and vehicles. A raffish mob gathered at the Treasury building in every conceivable kind of conveyance and proceeded to get drunk by the numbers. Out of one contingent of a thousand, only 75 reached the field, and all ambulances were badly overtaxed.

The affair was so scandalous that Stanton, who did not have to learn a lesson twice, gave Hammond his way about the ambulance corps. The surgeon, a man of prodigious force, went to work so vigorously that at Antietam the ambulance corps was a functioning entity, and its value steadily increased. It was one of the little-noticed innovations of the war; all modern military

medical services are modeled on Hammond's organization. After the war he became a famous neurologist and wrote successful novels.

After Antietam the phrase "All Quiet Along the Potomac" began to hit the headlines again. McClellan was busy at his favorite task of reorganization, and the only fighting was a little sniping across the river. Lincoln went up to see whether he could be persuaded to move, an event chronicled thus:

The President, accompanied by General M'Clellan, had a grand review of the Army of the Upper Potomac on 3rd October. His reception and that of General M'Clellan was intensely enthusiastic. The President commenced with General Burnside's corps, and proceeded to those of Generals Porter, Reynolds and Franklin, and the division of General Richardson, taking in the whole ground from the mouth of Antietam Creek to Bakersville.

The President returned to Washington from his visit to the army on Saturday night, 4th, and immediately had an interview with Mr. Stanton.

There is no hint here, nor was there in the rest of the press, that Lincoln's patience with the dilatory general was by this date wearing decidedly thin, or that McClellan was on his last chance. After the visit McClellan went to Philadelphia and was entertained by the ladies of the city at a champagne supper. He told them that the Emancipation Proclamation was an outrage.

Late in 1862, when Admiral D. D. Porter took over the Mississippi fleet, and it was transferred from its anomalous position under the War Department to navy administration, there began to appear on the rivers a new class of vessels. These were the "tinclads," altered from commercial river craft. Along their lower decks the first of these ships, like the one reproduced above, carried bales of hay; above they were armored with boiler iron, which made them safe against musketry, if not anything heavier.

Most of them mounted four, six, or eight 24-pound howitzers and had room for riflemen behind the upper bulwarks. The special feature of the tinclads was their light draft; some of them could work in as little as 16 inches of water, or as Porter put it, "run in a heavy dew." With this draft and their gunnery equipment they were used to patrol the Mississippi and its tributaries and to convoy transports and supply ships against guerilla bands and cavalry raiders, who had a habit of appearing suddenly to shoot up unarmed craft.

No ships in the war worked harder, fought harder, or had more adventures than these tinclads, and none received less publicity. There were 22 of them in service by the end of 1862 and 26 more were added the following year; and there was hardly a day until the end of the war when one of them

Ford near Shepherdstown, on the Potomac. Picket firing across the river

Tinclad in action on the Ohio

was not in action somewhere. But except at the beginning, when their oddity attracted one or two of the artist correspondents, their exploits remained buried in the official reports. Not even the name of the ship here is given.

Few transactions of the war attracted more attention than the shooting of "Bull" Nelson by General Jefferson C. Davis during Bragg's invasion of Kentucky. The scene was Louisville, where the two were trying to organize a defense, Nelson over Davis. The contemporary account tells how Nelson swore at Davis over some matter of the organization of his brigade. Davis asked Governor Morton of Indiana to accompany him to see Nelson, and then:

Gen. Davis. "Sir, you seemed to take advantage of your authority the other day."

Gen. Nelson (sneeringly and placing his hand to his ear) "Speak louder, I don't hear you very well."

Davis (in a louder tone) "You seemed to take advantage of your authority the other day."

Nelson (indignantly) "I don't know that I did, Sir."

Davis. "You threatened to arrest and send me out of the State under a provost guard."

The assassination of General Nelson by General Jefferson C. Davis

Nelson (striking Davis with the back of his hand twice in the face) "There, d — — n you, take that."

Davis (retreating) "This is not the last of it; you will hear from me again."

General Nelson then turned to Governor Morton, and said: "By G — d, did you come here also to insult me?"

Gov. Morton. "No, Sir, but I was requested to be present and listen to the conversation between you and General Davis."

Gen. Nelson (violently to the by-standers). "Did you hear the d — — — d rascal insult me?" and walked into the ladies' room.

In three minutes General Davis returned with a pistol he had borrowed of Captain Gibson, of Louisville, and walked toward the door that Nelson had passed through. He saw Nelson walking out of the parlor into the hall separating the main hall from the parlor. The two were face to face, and about ten yards apart, when General Davis drew his pistol and fired, the ball entering Nelson's heart or in the immediate vicinity.

Nelson was an immensely tall, strong man, who had been a naval lieutenant; it is hard to determine today just what made him fly out at Davis so. Davis was never brought to account for the shooting; he was a reasonably capable soldier who commanded a division, and then a corps, in Sherman's Atlanta campaign.

Perryville was the climax and the end of Bragg's invasion of Kentucky as Antietam was of Lee's invasion of Maryland. Actually, it was an accidental battle, brought on when some of Bragg's and Buell's vanguards started a contest for some pools of water, and both sides fed men in until major portions of the armies were engaged. The report, by "Our staff artist" has its Gothic aspects:

When M'Cook and Rousseau (Union generals) appeared before the town they found the immense forces of the enemy most advantageously posted to meet them. The rebels were posted on a long range of hills, extending in a crescent form from north to west. On these hills the rebel generals exhorted their soldiers to dye their colors deep in the blood of the enemy rather than surrender them.

We opened upon the enemy at 1 o'clock. The most sanguinary battle of the war commenced. The hills shook to their base, as one livid sheet of flame poured across them. Shell would whiz through the air, fall at the point of their aim, and burst, dealing death all around. Solid shot went screaming across the field, cutting great gaps through the ranks. Next come the

The Battle of Perryville, Kentucky, fought October 8, 1862

Destruction of a Rebel salt factory, on the coast of Florida, by the crew of United States bark *Kingfisher*

crash of musketry, quick, loud, and incessant. The noise of these guns blended with that of the artillery in tumultuous roar. Never, perhaps, was there a battle fought at so short a range, and never were fires so murderous and destructive. The battle had reached its height at 3. For an hour now it was a succession of advances and repulses. On the right a desperate attempt was made to flank the reinforcing column of M'Cook, which was partially successful, some of the new regiments wavering and staggering under the galling cross-fire poured upon them.

The first advantage gained by the enemy in the centre was by one of those acts of perfidy which they have never been slow to exhibit. A rebel Colonel, with National uniform on, advanced along to the centre, where the brave Indianians were exposed, and shouted "Hurrah for the old Hoosier boys!" He was met as a comrade, and by deception the rebels were permitted to advance to within a few yards of our men. A most unexpected and murderous fire was poured upon us from two sides, without our regiment even returning it. The Indiana boys were of course stunned and thrown into temporary confusion. The battle having raged fiercely now for

five hours, and the men being exhausted with slaughter, just as night began to conceal the field of death and blood, the combatants ceased their awful work. Our troops fell back a short distance under cover of the woods, worn and exhausted with their hot day's work.

The more purple the prose, the poorer the report. It sounds singularly like the account of a defeat; actually, Perryville was not a particularly bloody battle, as Civil War battles went, and was not a defeat at all. The best the Confederates could claim was a draw, and after the battle was over, Bragg retreated toward Tennessee.

Moreover, there are some very striking omissions. Buell, who was in command, is not mentioned at all, and the only generals who are mentioned are McCook and Rousseau. But the army knew then, and history has confirmed since that the master figure of Perryville was a young general of division named P. H. Sheridan, who held the center against a heavy attack, then counterattacked, driving the rebels

The Army of the Potomac. A sharpshooter on picket duty.

Convalescent soldiers passing through Washington to join their regiments

right through Perryville. It made him a marked man in the service, if not with the public; but the battle was fatal to Buell, relieved later by W. S. Rosecrans.

There is little historical record of the immense damage done by the Union navy along the Atlantic coast of the Southern states, because the individual incidents had so little importance. But there was a steady, exhausting drain, not from the blockade alone. Armed ferryboats and double-enders pushed up the rivers, destroying mills, bridges, railroads, carrying off cotton when there was any to carry off, and making organized life virtually impossible within the range of their guns and landing parties.

Along the more open coast of Florida it was the same. Indeed, it may fairly be said that after Fernandina was occupied and the coastal descents began, Florida took virtually no part in the war. "The whole coast of Florida is lined with these works of a smaller size," says the text. "This one, when finished, would have been capable of making five hundred bushels a day, at $10 a bushel."

The dome of the Capitol was still incomplete when these convalescents marched past. Contemporary comment:

The subject struck me when I saw it as one of interest in the present period. Washington just now is very dry and dusty, as I have indicated in the sketch. The soldiers were under escort. This is the military custom. They were on their way to the railway station near the capital, and belonged to different regiments, representing nearly all the States, and were in every variety of garb. You will perceive they are not in Broadway fashion. The soldier who has been in service is a different looking object from the trim gent he was when he left home.

The thinned regiments of the Army of the Potomac which returned from the Peninsula in September last have been considerably recruited by the arrival of convalescent soldiers from hospital. Wounds have been healed and the bracing air of October has dispelled the fevers engendered by the Chickahominy malaria.

Maybe so; but one of the charges against McClellan was precisely the number of men he had on leave and sick report. It once caused Lincoln to remark that: "Sending that man reinforcements is like shoveling flies across a room."

The removal of McClellan in favor of Ambrose Burnside got all the space the press could afford. *Harper's Weekly* had this to say:

The President appears to have determined on the step in the last week of October; but for reasons which can readily be conceived it was not carried into effect until the 8th inst. A dispatch from General Halleck to the Secretary of War, bearing date October 28, explains the reasons which led the President to act. After the Battle of Antietam General Halleck first urged, then ordered General M'Clellan to move across the Potomac. He did not move for three weeks, and, in General Halleck's opinion, no good excuse existed for his disobedience and delay.

General M'Clellan's friends, who are legion, will urge in his defense that a General in command of an army of 200,-000 men, and responsible not only for his own success but for their lives, is the best judge of when and how he should move, and can not be bound to obey the orders of persons at a distance from the scene of action, and without direct personal responsibility in the matter. It will doubtless further be urged that, however slow General M'Clellan may have been during the first three weeks of October, he was moving with remarkable celerity when the order for his removal was handed to him. Many other good arguments may be advanced in vindication of the displaced General, but they are not likely to be much heard of just now. Both the people and the army are too intent on the great work of suppressing the rebellion to trouble themselves about side issues. After the war there will be time to inquire into and pass judgment upon them, and

General McClellan surrendering the command of the Army of the Potomac to General Burnside

then, if injustice has been done to M'Clellan, he will probably be elected President.

Meanwhile it is a source of unmixed satisfaction to know that the Army of the Potomac is led by a man like Burnside, a soldier who to the greatest military skill unites dash, energy, and the prestige of success, and a man of the most exalted character and the noblest heart. The country unites in the cry, "God speed Burnside!"

It is curious to note that McClellan's subsequent presidential campaign was in the works as early as this; or at least being put in the works for him. It may also be noted that Mr. A. R. Waud, who made the picture of the relief, was almost certainly not an eyewitness. Those who were are agreed that it was snowing gently and have commented on the line of white flakes across the new commander's bridge of whisker.

The farewell to his officers, which McClellan made as much like Wash-ington's as possible, drew this kind of notice:

Accompanied by his officers and escort, a magnificent cavalcade, he rode off to take a last farewell of his troops. The infantry and cavalry attached to his head-quarters were tastefully displayed on an adjacent hill. M'Clellan rode along the lines, and as he passed enthusiastic cheers spontaneously arose from the ranks. The soldiers could not restrain their controlling admiration for their General.

Having passed through the lines of all the troops in the vicinity, General M'Clellan turned his horse's head to go back to head-quarters, where he intended proceeding to the train. Now was witnessed the most affecting scene of all. He was going away from them — he was already gone. The moment that they fully realized it, all those soldiers, animated by one universal impulse, ran after him, some weeping aloud, and shouted in the most touching and affecting manner, "Fetch him back, fetch him back!" and "Oh, come back to us, come back to us, M'Clellan!"

McClellan's adieux to his officers at Warrenton, Virginia

This was probably every bit true. The morale of the Army of the Potomac, which sank dangerously during the brief and unhappy reign of Burnside, was recovered under Hooker, but no other commander ever inspired the affection with which the men regarded McClellan.

When Burnside took command he said he did not feel competent to command so large an army, and he rapidly proved it. The two armies lay on the upper waters of the Rappahannock; the plan laid before Lincoln by the new general was for a march down the left bank of the river, then a strike through Fredericksburg, straight at Richmond. Lincoln thought it would succeed "if you move quickly."

But Burnside did not move quickly; and when he reached Fredericksburg there were no pontoons. The result was that by the time he was ready to cross, the Confederates had occupied the hills behind the town, and were quite ready when Burnside forced a crossing. He could think of nothing better than ordering an assault up those heights in the face of men in trenches and behind stone walls, reported thus:

We publish an account of the bombardment of Fredericksburg, and the successfull crossing of the river. On the following day, Saturday, 13th, the fight was renewed. It is stated that 40,000 men of our army were engaged against a large force of rebels. Franklin, on the left, gained some ground. Sumner, on the right and centre, attacked the first line of the rebel defenses, but was repulsed. The loss of life was very great. On Sunday, 14th, the battle was not renewed. There was some artillery firing in the morning, but it ceased about noon. During the storm and darkness of Monday night General Burnside succeeded in making good his retreat across the Rappahannock without attracting the attention of the enemy. The artillery was first moved over, the infantry bringing up the rear, and reached the north bank a short time after daylight."

This is good straight reporting, with no attempt to conceal what had happened, and the pictorial coverage is

81

The bombardment of Fredericksburg by the Army of the Potomac

Thanksgiving in camp

The assault of Marye's Heights at Fredericksburg

Winter quarters in camp. The inside of a hut

equally good. For almost the first time a charge is shown being made in the way they really were made. Incidentally, it should be noted that the bombardment of Fredericksburg was not an act of wanton barbarity but the classical method of winning a river crossing when the enemy is in force on the other side.

In the files of the weeklies there is no sign of the something like despair that descended on the Army of the Potomac. They were more concerned with a "Cabinet imbroglio" in which a caucus of Senators voted lack of confidence in Secretary Seward and asked for his removal, with Banks at New Orleans and with Emancipation. A tiny cartoon shows a back view of "Mr. Nobody, the man responsible for the Fredericksburg disaster," and it is not until January 17 that an editorial takes up military affairs under the title of "Have We a General?"

Too long to give in full, it regrets McClellan: "Such opportunities as he enjoyed have seldom been vouch-safed to any one in any country at any time. And it is still an open question whether or not he made the most of them." Burnside gets something of a brush-off, with praise for the energy and daring shown in his operations in the Carolina sounds, and the attempt to storm Fredericksburg. They "were not at all in the M'Clellan style." But there is doubt about his foresight and power of combination—in other words about his brains.

Of the western generals, Grant has been "fortunate. Whether his record will bear the test of inquiry, is a question yet undetermined." Sherman, then making the Haines' Bluff attempt on Vicksburg (an accompanying news dispatch said he had probably taken it), is no more than "a capable officer." S. R. Curtis gets praise for his record in Missouri, but most particularly for his administrative capacity. "Those who know General Banks expect more of him, and believe that before this war ends he will rank high among its heroes."

**But:**

At the present, however, the most promising of our soldiers is General William S. Rosecrans. He spent six weeks at Nashville in concentrating his forces, and accumulating equipments and supplies for the campaign. He moved on 29th December, and after five days' desperate fighting, completely defeated, and "drove" the rebel army under Bragg. As a strategist Rosecrans has proved himself second to none.

This was the editorial reflection of the terrific Battle of Stone River, on which the dispatches had just come in. If it shows a certain distortion, a lack of awareness of what really happened at Stone River, it can only be justified by the fact that the dispatches were official, signed by William S. Rosecrans himself, and contained the following passage:

"General Thomas was partially surprised, thrown into confusion, and driven back."

History has taken a very different view of Thomas' stand at Stone River, where it was McCook, not he, who was surprised; and of his stand in the council of war that night, when Rosecrans wanted to give up and retreat. But there was no corrective; the correspondents, for some reason, failed to cover the battle, and so did the artists. It is the only great battle of the war that received no pictorial reporting at all, and very little from the newspaper men.

Meanwhile the Army of the Potomac was building itself huts for winter quarters north of the Rappahannock, and was in thoroughly bad shape. When a cheer for Burnside was called for on parade, the men hooted instead, and two of the generals went secretly to the White House to tell Lincoln that it would be "dangerous folly" to attempt another campaign while the men were in such a mood.

About the same time word reached Washington that Burnside had ordered three days' rations cooked in preparation for another movement. Lincoln told him to hold it up until he had come to Washington for a secret conference.

At this conference Burnside defended himself against the charge of low morale and produced figures to show that both the number and percentage of absentees had declined since McClellan's day. Still there were ominous rumors, and Lincoln tried to get Halleck to go down to the army and find out what was wrong. Halleck would not, and matters hung fire while Lincoln tried to find another remedy.

Nothing at all of this leaked to the press. Maybe the reporters of those days didn't have as many friends as they do now.

In December, 1862, the *Monitor* was caught in a gale off Hatteras while moving down in tow of the *Rhode Island* for a campaign off Charleston. This is the account of an officer:

From ten to eleven P.M. the water gained rapidly. It was now known for certain that she had sprung a leak. The storm was at its height, the waves striking and passing over the *Monitor,* burying her completely for the instant, while for a few minutes nothing could be seen of her from the *Rhode Island* but the upper part of her turret, surrounded by foam. The projecting armor is undoubtedly the cause of the leak, as it extended aft thirty-two feet and forward fourteen. This constantly striking the water with the force that it did, and the immense weight of ammunition in the hull, must have separated one from the other, thus causing a leak from which she filled and sank.

She was now found to be fast sinking, and a consultation was held whether to abandon her or not. The engineer, entering at the moment, reported that the water in the ward-room was waist deep; that it was gaining rapidly, and that in less than two hours she must go down. This decided Captain Bankhead to save the lives of his men rather than lose both. Signals of distress were now ordered to be made to the *Rhode Island;* and while these were preparing Captain Bankhead shouted, "Who'll cut the hawser?" "I will," answered Mr. Stodder, the Master; and taking a hatchet, he, at imminent peril of being washed overboard, succeeded in severing the hawser.

Several of the crew and some of the officers found a watery grave by being washed overboard. . . .

and those left had a terrible time reaching *Rhode Island* in the latter's boats, and one of the boats got lost in the night and was not found till morning.

A certain special interest attaches to this contemporary picture: *Monitor* is shown nowhere else with the curious double funnel drawn in this picture, and it is mentioned in no account, but the artist probably had some reason for drawing it that way.

After the Emancipation Proclamation, the weeklies seldom missed an opportunity to remind their readers that slavery had become one of the main issues of the war. They did it with a certain amount of subtlety, as in the case on the next page.

Fredericksburg and Stone River marked a turning point in one sense. It was not until after these battles that ads for artificial legs began appearing in the papers; later in the war these ads became more and more numerous and were presently joined by advertising for artificial arms, as well as for metal badges that would permit identification if the wearer were killed or wounded.

The winter of 1862-1863 marked a low point in Union morale. The fall elections had gone against Lincoln;

The wreck of the ironclad *Monitor*

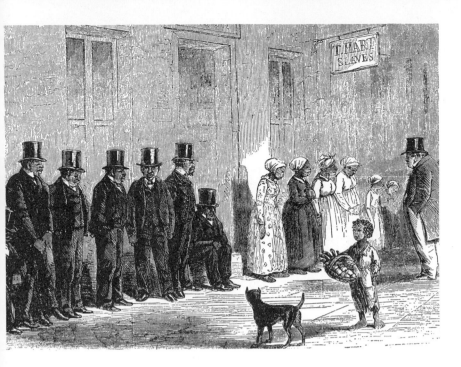

A slave pen at New Orleans. Before the auction. A sketch of the past

then came the dreadful blow of Fredericksburg, followed by the news of Sherman's defeat at Haines' Bluff, and the loss of Galveston. There were four gunboats in Galveston Harbor—a former revenue cutter, a 90-day gunboat, and two converted ferryboats. The town was occupied by a single regiment.

"Prince John" Magruder, the Confederate commander in Texas, fitted three steamers with cotton-bale armor, filled them with riflemen, and on the night of January 1 brought them close alongside *Harriet Lane,* the revenue cutter, at the same time filling the streets with soldiers, who quickly captured the regiment. Everyone on the cutter's deck was shot down and she was carried by boarding. The contemporary account says:

> When morning dawned, signals were sent up from the flag-ship, which were responded to by all the gun-boats except the *Harriet Lane,* and now it was that the Commodore first discovered that she had

fallen into the hands of the enemy. The light also revealed the position of the enemy's fleet, and his preparations for an attack from the shore with artillery and riflemen.

Unfortunately *Westfield,* one of the ferryboats, was hard aground, under the shore guns. Commander Renshaw, in charge of the little squadron, set her afire, but the flames spread so fast that she blew up, killing him and a couple of other officers; whereupon Lieutenant-Commander Law of the gunboat *Owasco,* as senior surviving officer, steamed out of the harbor with his remaining ships as fast as he could.

The weekly's story is full and fairly accurate, except at the beginning and the end. The first is understandable; no one on the Northern side at the time could know precisely how it started. But the end of the account was fudged to cover up for Law—or perhaps he covered up for himself, and it took time to get at the facts.

Attack of the Rebels upon our gunboat flotilla at Galveston, Texas, January 1, 1863: *Harriet Lane,* Rebel gunboats, *Owasco, Westfield* being blown up, *Mary Boardman*

Sherman's assault at Haines' Bluff

There was no attempt to cover up the fact that Sherman had failed at Haines' Bluff. The story reads:

General Sherman's repulse at Vicksburg was complete. The entire force, under General M'Clernand, re-embarked on 3d on transports, closely followed by the rebel advance, which, coming in range of the gun-boats, were driven back with severe loss. Our loss was six hundred killed, one thousand five hundred wounded, and one thousand missing.

A council of war was held on 4th on board the *Tigress*. Admiral Porter, Major-Generals Sherman and M'Clernand, with the Generals of the division of the army in Kentucky were present. It was determined at this council that it would be folly to attempt any thing further against Vicksburg with the present force. It was, therefore, deemed expedient that the campaign should be abandoned for the present.

A telegraphic dispatch from General Pemberton to the rebel Secretary of War, dated on the 8th, says that all the Union troops have gone up the river; that there were only seven gun-boats between Vicksburg and Milliken's Bend, and that the city was being strengthened every day, and could be maintained against all attacks. The rebel Generals Pemberton and Price are in command there. The rebel forces

have been reinforced to the extent of sixty thousand men. They have an artillery force of one hundred and sixty guns in battery, besides a large number of field-pieces.

The estimate of the enemy's force is high, but that is usual in war. The really fascinating point is how the *Harper's Weekly* reporter knew about that telegram from Pemberton to Richmond; it stands in the official records and is exactly as stated. It is, of course, possible that the wire was tapped somewhere; we know that later in the campaign Grant was getting most of the Confederate messages.

In January, after Halleck had refused to conduct an inquiry into the affairs of the Army of the Potomac, Burnside decided to have a try at getting around Lee's position by marching up the Rappahannock for a crossing behind the Confederate flank, the march to be made at night. It began to rain during the day before the march and continued steadily all night.

The night's rain had made deplorable havoc with the roads. The nature of the

Skirmishing in the advance

Distributing the mails

Rush to a haystack.

General

Life in the Army

On the march in a storm.

Croops fording a stream.

Wild Cat.

Clearing the Road.

of the Cumberland

Fruitless attempt of the Army of the Potomac to move toward the Rappahannock

Paying off the teamsters in the Army of the Potomac

upper geologic deposits of the region affords unequaled elements for bad roads. The sand makes the soil pliable, the clay makes it sticky, and the two together form a road out of which, when it rains, the bottom drops, but which is at the same time so tenacious that extrication from its clutch is all but impossible.

The utmost effort was put forth to get pontoons enough into position to construct a bridge or two. Double and triple teams of horses and mules were harnessed to each pontoon-boat. It was in vain. Long, powerful ropes were then attached to the teams, and a hundred and fifty men were put to the task on each boat. The effort was but little more successful. Night arrived, but the pontoons could not be got up. The rebels had discovered what was up, and the pickets on the opposite bank called over to ours that they "would come over to-morrow and help us build the bridge."

That night the troops again bivouacked in the same position in the woods they had held the night before. The men were in the woods, which afforded them some shelter from the wind and rain. On the following morning a whisky ration, provided by the judicious forethought of General Burnside, was on hand for them.

Thursday morning dawned upon another day of storm and rain. An indescribable chaos of pontoons, wagons and artillery encumbered the road down to the river—artillery "stalled" in the mud—ammunition trains mired by the way. Horses and mules dropped down dead, exhausted with the effort.

The army returned sadly to its camps, more depressed than ever, and the operation passed into contemporary accounts as "the Mud March."

Meanwhile there was action on the Mississippi. *Queen of the West*, one of the Ellet rams, ran through the Vicksburg batteries to take station off the mouth of the Red River and cut the Confederate supply lines running to Vicksburg and Port Hudson. She was brilliantly successful at first but, going up the river, got under a battery which put a shot through her that cut her steam pipe, and she ran aground while trying to get down on the current. Her crew abandoned her in boats and on floating bales of cotton.

## The loss of the *Queen of the West*

Among those aboard was Joseph McCullagh, one of the most famous of war correspondents, both reporter and artist. He was one of those who escaped on a cotton bale and promptly furnished an accurate account, accompanied by an equally accurate picture.

In the meantime the ironclad *Indianola* had also run the batteries. She was a peculiar craft, built by Joseph Brown of Cincinnati, with casemates fore and aft, each containing two heavy guns. It was not enough. The Confederates quickly repaired *Queen of the West* and brought her upstream in company with a ram of their own and some smaller craft containing sharpshooters. On a dark night they attacked *Indianola*. She fired her guns but could only bear two in each direction, and in the murk they missed. Reloading was an operation that took nearly five minutes with that type of piece; before the ironclad could get off many more shots, she had been rammed several times from astern, her wheels were disabled and she was driven into the bank, where she surrendered.

The only account of the affair given by the press was Admiral Porter's dispatch, which said the loss could be "traced to non-compliance with my instructions." There was no editorial comment; losses were beginning to be taken with a certain amount of sophistication.

The loss of *Indianola*, however, gave rise to one of the most diverting incidents of the war. She had not been in rebel hands for 24 hours when Porter had a dummy ironclad constructed on an old flatboat, with logs for armor and guns and two tall funnels made out of pork barrels, at the base of each of which was placed a large kettle full of tar and oakum, set alight to make smoke.

She could only drift with the current, but as none of the ironclads could do much more, this made no difference in her appearance.

After passing the batteries at night, and defying all the guns at Vicksburg, she lay a whole day opposite the canal—the rebels trying in vain to sink her, and never for a moment discovering their error—when she got into the current again, and "sailed in" on the *Queen of the West* (which vessel

The United States gunboat *Indianola* (ironclad) running the blockade at Vicksburg

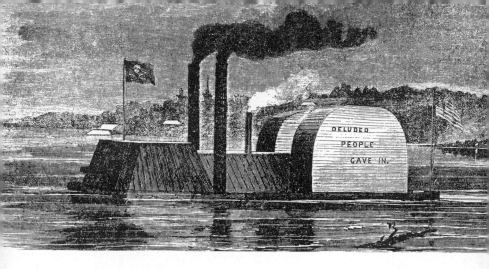

Admiral Porter's dummy frightening the Rebels at Vicksburg

Bayou navigation in Dixie

The Rams *Switzerland* and *Lancaster* running the blockade at Vicksburg

had just arrived at Warrenton), when it was amusing to see the rebel rammer clap on steam and vamose the ranche. Indeed, she never stopped until she came to the *Indianola;* but finding that the grim monster was after her, they applied the torch, and blew her and every thing in her to atoms. It was a great relief to all of us here, for we could imagine the damage the *Indianola* could have effected on the river in case she had been saved.

The effort of *Lancaster* and *Switzerland,* two more of the Ellet rams, to run the Vicksburg batteries, really belongs to a later date but is placed here because it belongs essentially to the same campaign. Farragut had come up from the gulf with two of his ocean ships to blockade the Red, but he wanted one of the rams because of their speed, higher than any other ships on the river. *Lancaster* was a rather old ship and did not make it, being hit in the engines and set on fire.

This was the period of the attempt to work through to the rear of Vicksburg by means of the bayous of the Yazoo delta, which became deep and wide enough to admit considerable ship traffic in the floods of the early part of the year. The weekly's artist caught two of the transports at it, and submitted a picture accompanied by some purple prose about the landscape.

After the "Mud March" the state of morale in the Army of the Potomac could no longer be concealed, and was even exaggerated in the press, to the point of reporting that the army was on the edge of mutiny. There were already a good many rumors going around about General Joseph Hooker, who had tried to put through a plan of campaign all his own at the beginning of the Fredericksburg operation, and was pretty much at odds with Burnside. Henry Raymond of the New York *Times* even suggested to Burnside that Hooker might lead a mutiny.

Major General Hooker, commanding
the Army of the Potomac

Burnside replied that if Hooker tried
it, he would swing before sundown,
but he was disturbed, and the vague
murmurings in part of the press about
a military dictatorship being necessary
did nothing to calm him. On January
23 he telegraphed the President asking for an interview, and went up to
Washington with papers.

The papers were orders dismissing
from the service Generals Newton and
Cochrane (whom Burnside had now
identified as the pair who earlier described the poor state of the army to
Lincoln) with Brooks and Hooker.
Generals Franklin, W. F. Smith,
Sturgis, Ferrero, and a staff colonel
who had somehow incurred Burnside's displeasure were to be dismissed
from the Army of the Potomac. Unless
these steps were taken, Burnside would
resign. Lincoln accepted the resigna-
tion and with some doubts appointed
Hooker in Burnside's place.

The press does not seem to have
caught a hint of the behind-the-scenes
story. Gossip columnists were not yet
in existence, and there were fewer
managed leaks than there are today.
The reporting of the change in command was entirely colorless, unaccom-
panied by editorial comment. The
biographies of Hooker that presently
appeared were equally colorless except
for an explanation of how he got the
name "Fighting Joe":

On one occasion, after a battle, in which
General Hooker's men had distinguished
themselves for their fighting qualities, thus
adding to the fame of their commander,
a dispatch to the New York Associated
Press was received at the office of one of
the principal agencies announcing the
fact. One of the copyists, wishing to show
in an emphatic manner that the commander was really a fighting man, placed
over the head of the manifold copies of
the dispatch the words "Fighting Joe
Hooker. Of course this heading went to
nearly every newspaper office of the country, through the various agencies, and
was readily adopted by the editors and
printed in their journals. The *sobriquet*
was also adopted by the army and by the
press, and is now well known to all the
world. Thus an unpretending, innocent
copyist, unaware that he was making history, prefixed to the General's name a title
that will live forever in the annals of the
country. But it appears that General
Hooker does not like the title.

All the same, Hooker began moving
things around at once, and as he
moved them, the morale of the army
improved. Three of the older corps
commanders were either moved out
or resigned. Hooker made an effort
to cut down on the wagon train by
introducing pack mules instead, but
after some experiment, it was found
that didn't work. On the lower levels
he improved by introducing a badge
for each corps — a clover leaf for the
II, a Maltese cross for the V and so on
— and this helped matters. He insti-

A wedding in the Army of the Potomac

tuted a system of regular drills, which no one seems to have thought of before. Also, while in winter quarters he granted furloughs much more freely than either of his predecessors, but he accompanied this by compiling careful lists of absentees and checking up on them, something that McClellan had never done. By the end of March the total number of absentees from the army had been reduced by a half.

Very little of this made the press at the time. It was not that the reporting was bad but that minor details of army life were considered subjects for pictorial rather than verbal reporting and there was little in them that could be reported pictorially. The correspondents confined themselves to narratives of events and pictures of nature; a quite different school of thought than the reporting of today. One of Hooker's morale-building steps was to lose no opportunity for festivities. The *Weekly* reports a wedding:

In a hollow square formed by the troops a canopy was erected, an altar of drums, officers grouped on either side of this. On General Hooker's arrival the band played Hail to the Chief, and on the approach of the bridal party the Wedding March. It was rather cold, windy, and threatening snow, altogether tending to produce a slight pink tinge on the noses present; but the ladies bore it with courage, and looked, to the unaccustomed eyes of the soldiers, like real angels in their light clothing. To add to the dramatic force of the scene, the rest of the brigade were drawn up in line of battle not more than a mile away to repel an expected attack. Few persons are wedded under more romantic circumstances than Nellie Lammond and Captain De Hart. He could not get leave of absence, so she came down like a brave girl, and married him in camp. After the wedding was a dinner, a ball, fire-works, etc., and on the whole it eclipsed entire an opera at the Academy of Music in dramatic effect and reality.

One hopes the marriage turned out well.

The new monitors had begun to arrive at Port Royal, and it was proposed to use them in a naval attack on Charleston and Fort Sumter. Serious doubts were expressed by many, including John Ericsson, about the ability of the monitors to stand up under steady fire from forts. To test the matter the monitor *Montauk* was taken into the Ogeechee River, where

99

The destruction of the *Nashville* by the ironclad monitor *Montauk*

the English-built raider *Nashville* was lying under the guns of Fort McAllister. She shelled *Nashville* into a blazing wreck and the return fire from the fort only dislodged a couple of bolts in the pilothouse.

This was license enough to send Admiral S. F. DuPont into the entrance of Charleston harbor with seven monitors, the broadside ironclad *New Ironsides,* and the turtle-back ironclad *Keokuk.* The result:

The attack on Charleston has been made, and has failed. Admiral DuPont has withdrawn, after losing one vessel, being perfectly satisfied that it was hopeless to renew the contest with the force he has. With an ingenuity and industry worthy of a better cause, the rebels have so obstructed the approaches to the port of Charleston that no vessel can enter until the obstructions — a combination of piles, stakes, chains, ropes, nets, and torpedoes — have been removed. Over three hundred guns, carrying missiles of the largest and most destructive character, poured an incessant hail upon the eight gun-boats which vainly endeavored to bombard Fort Sumter on the 7th inst.

Each person draws his own inferences and forms his own opinion of the affair, according to his hopes and views, and the temper of his mind. The most obvious of all inferences is that it insures an indefinite prolongation of the war. Had we destroyed Fort Sumter and occupied Charleston there would have been good ground for expecting the early collapse of the rebellion. As it is, the rebels will be encouraged to persevere in their rebellion, while we shall merely renew our preparations for another and possibly a more successful attack. It will, however, take several months to build new ironclads.

After the loss of *Indianola* the question of blockading the Red River came up again, and this time Farragut decided to run up from New Orleans with his ocean-going ships. He had three of the big sloops, three gunboats, and the side-wheel frigate *Mississippi*. Only his flagship and an accompanying gunboat got through; the other two sloops were driven back disabled, while *Mississippi* ran hard aground under the guns and had to be evacuated and burned.

Contemporary accounts are mostly straight narratives from eyewitnesses aboard the ships, a method greatly favored in the reporting of the period; but the general impression given is of a defeat, and the Confederates duly regarded it as a victory. This is another case of the strategic myopia visible in the accounts of Fort Donelson and other early operations. Farragut lost a valuable ship and barely got through; but he had achieved his object, supplies ceased to flow down the Red, and when Port Hudson was blockaded on the land side as well, it was ultimately forced to surrender.

The pictorial account of the passage of the forts by Artist Hamilton, is one of the most imaginary efforts of the war. Precisely the reason the ships had so much trouble was that Farragut's *Hartford* was the only ship that could see where she was going. It was a

The Union ironclad fleet, commanded by Admiral Dupont, opening fire upon Fort Sumter, Charleston harbor, Tuesday, April 7

Bombardment of Port Hudson by Admiral Farragut's fleet, March 14-15

Destruction of the U.S. steamer *Mississippi*, Saturday night, March 14, in the Mississippi River, below Port Hudson. Explosion of the magazine

dark, overcast night, chosen for that reason, and as soon as the ships opened fire, the river became so enshrouded in smoke that the pilots lost sight of the winding channel. The other two sloops were hit when they touched ground, and all through the battle both sides were firing at gun flash. Moreover *Mississippi* never got round the point of land opposite the fort and was not all in flames, lined up with the rest, as she is shown. This was clear even from accounts written at the time.

A correspondent has sent us a sketch of an event which caused great excitement in Dayton, Ohio, where Mr. Vallandigham resides. It appears that early on the morning of the 5th of May a detachment of soldiers sent by Gen. Burnside travelled by a special train from Cincinnati to Dayton, with an order to arrest Mr. Vallandigham. The soldiers were obliged to batter down two or three doors of his house before they reached him. His friends rang the fire bells, and an attempt was made by the people to rescue him, but without success. The mob then proceeded to the Dayton *Journal* office, and set it on fire, remaining on the spot till it was entirely consumed. The telegraph wires were also cut. The damage by fire amounted to $40,000. Mr. Vallandigham was taken to Cincinnati, where an inquiry was held, but the result was not made public.

The official charges against him are: That on or about the 1st of May at Mount Vernon, Ohio, he publicly addressed a large meeting of citizens, declaring that the present war is an injurious, cruel and unnecessary war—a war not being waged for the preservation of the Union, but for the purpose of crushing out liberty and establishing a despotism — a war for the freedom of the blacks and enslaving of the whites; and that, if the Administration had so wished, the war could have been honorably terminated; that peace might have been honorably obtained by listening to the proposed intermediation of France; that propositions by which the Southern States could be won back and be guaranteed their rights under the Con-

*Above:* Arrest of the Honorable C. L. Vallandigham at Dayton, Ohio, May 5.
*Below:* Mr. Vallandigham delivered at the lines to the officer of the Rebel picket guard

stitution were rejected the day before the battle of Fredericksburg. He is also charged with having said that order No. 38 of Gen. Burnside was a base usurpation of arbitrary authority, and the sooner the people informed the minions of usurpated power that they will not submit to such restrictions the better. He declared also his purpose to defeat an attempt to build up a monarchy upon the ruins of our free Government, and, that he believed the men in power were trying to establish a despotism.

Thus the weekly on the arrest of the famous Copperhead, which made such a stir in its day, a good and objective account. The riot that followed demonstrated an amount of Copperhead sentiment that is not generally realized today, and probably had something to do with the Confederate attempt to promote the setting up of a Northwest Confederacy to bring the war to an end. But there were other issues also. The journal thought editorially:

There can be very little question but his imprisonment for months, and perhaps years, in a military fortress would make a martyr of him, and would rally to his side, for the sake of liberty and free speech, an immense number of sympathizers. Arresting seditious talkers implies a fear that the people have not sense or strength of mind enough to resist the appeals of sedition.

Lincoln was, of course, perfectly aware of this, even if Burnside was not. But he was also aware, which the press was not, that to order Vallandigham's release would be to disavow the act of his military subordinate, for which there was, after all, a certain amount of justification. It was these considerations that led to his solution of having Vallandigham deposited within the Confederate lines. Nobody offered the slightest objection.

It was on May 6 that there began to come off the wires the news that made Lincoln stagger so that he had to be helped down the War Department steps: the dreadful news of the Battle of Chancellorsville. Not even Second Bull Run or Fredericksburg produced such depression at the head of the government, principally because the hopes were higher there. The President had seen for himself how the army had recovered its morale, how well it was equipped. The bulk of the men were veterans; the numerical strength was impressive. And now this army, after three days of fighting, was "safely encamped" north of the Rappahannock, where it started from. "My God! My God! What will the country say?" said Lincoln.

What the country did say through the weekly was:

On the 28th, 29th and 30th April General Hooker crossed the Rappahannock at various fords from 10 to 20 miles above Fredericksburg, and drove in the rebel pickets, advancing his army to a small village called Chancellorsville, near the residence of a Mr. Chancellor. A day or two previously General Stoneman, with a large cavalry force, had been sent to make

The libertine foiled

*Above left:* Bridges and rifle pits at United States ford. *Above right:* The 8th Pennsylvania Cavalry crossing at Ely's Ford. *Below:* Russell's brigade (1st Division, VI Army Corps) crossing the Rappahannock in pontoons to storm the Rebel works

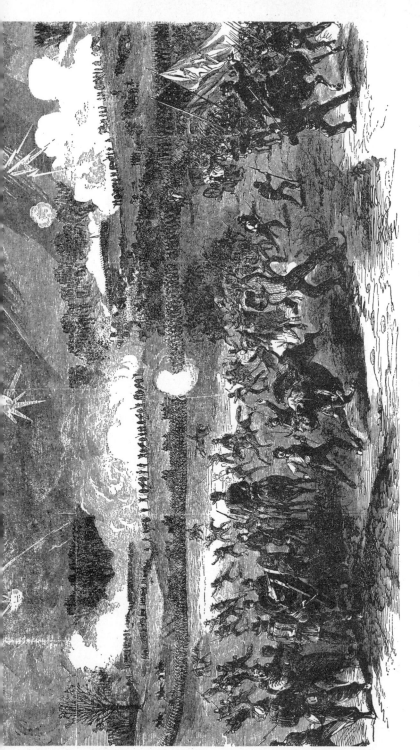

The battles at Chancellorsville. Couch's corps forming a line of battle to cover the retreat of the XI Corps, May 2, 1863

a grand detour by way of the Upper Rapidan and the southern part of Orange and Spotsylvania counties, with a view of cutting the railroad between Richmond and Fredericksburg in the neighborhood of Milford. General Hooker's advance took the rebels by surprise, and compelled them to come out of their intrenchments and attack the Union army. Withdrawing the bulk of his army from the heights above Fredericksburg, the rebel General made his first attack on Friday afternoon, another on Saturday, and a third on Sunday. These various fights appear to have been bloody and indecisive. Fortune varied, as usual in the great battles of the war; at times we drove the enemy, and at times they drove us; one day we took some guns and prisoners, and the next we lost some. But on Monday, 4th, General Sedgwick, who had stormed the heights of Fredericksburg when the rebels withdrew the bulk of their force from that point, was obliged to give way. General Longstreet, who is said to have brought up reinforcements to the rebels, attacked him fiercely, and finally drove him across the river, with a loss of some 6000 men. On the following day General Lee, flushed by success, threw his whole army on General Hooker, and compelled him also to withdraw his army across the Rappahannock. Of the results of General Stoneman's raid, which was a part of the general plan, we have as yet no intelligence that is worth repeating. He should by this time have succeeded in cutting the railroad, so as to prevent the transmission of supplies, reinforcements and amunition to General Lee. Comment on this event would as yet be premature.

Comment was, in fact, never made at all; other events inviting it piled in too fast. But even without comment, this is a notably poor piece of reporting, chiefly because the field men appear to have let the editors down by not getting the facts straight, even though the battle was somewhat confusing.

There was nothing at all indecisive about the fighting on Saturday, May 2; this was the day when Jackson got onto the flank of the XI Corps, drove it in, and almost rolled up the Union Army. Neither was Sunday, May 3, particularly indecisive; this was the day when Hooker's position was so driven in that there was nothing left for him to do but recross the river.

Sedgwick, whose corps had only been used at Fredericksburg as a feint, was not "forced to give way." He held his position until the attack was beaten into the ground and then made his retreat in good order. His loss was not 6000 men but 4593. It was not Longstreet who attacked him but Early; Longstreet's corps was not on the field at all. After Sedgwick had retreated, Lee did not "throw his whole army on" Hooker; there was no fighting to speak of on May 5, except a little rear-guard bickering.

Stoneman's raid, which got mired and never reached the Confederate rear at all, was not intended primarily to cut the railroad; both sides knew perfectly well that such a break as a raiding force of cavalry could make would have only a temporary effect, and during that time the army could live off its fat.

The errors of omission are equally striking. In spite of the fact that the editors seem not unwilling to confess defeat, as witness the lines about Sedgwick, there is not a word about the rout of the XI Corps under Jackson's flank attack. The fact that Hooker got a terrible blow on the head when a cannon ball went through a porch pillar against which he was leaning is not mentioned. Neither is the sacrificial charge of the Pennsylvania cavalry, which stopped Jackson just long enough to allow the Union to get some artillery into position and save the army. Nor is the work of that artillery. In fact, all through the war the artillery was neglected by the correspondents; it was only when historians began to

Splendid Advance of Sykes's Regulars.

Centre of our Line of Battle

Steam-Mill used as a Medical Depot.

The battles at Chancellorsville

study the record and get opinions from the other side that it was realized that more than anything else it was the Union guns that won the war.

All in all, the accounts of Chancellorsville by the Northern press bore comparatively little resemblance to reality. This makes it all the stranger that the pictorial coverage was very complete and remarkably good. (It is marked, incidentally, by the first appearance of a new field artist, Thomas Nast.) The error about the rout of the XI Corps was corrected two weeks later, though not in terms that showed any great understanding of what had happened:

The German regiments returned the fire for a short time with spirit, manifesting a disposition to fight valiantly. But at the time when all encouragement to the men was needed, then some officer of the division fell back to the rear, leaving his men alone. At the same time General Devens, commanding the First division, was unhorsed and badly wounded in his foot by a musket-ball. Thus losing at a critical moment the inspiring influence of the immediate presence of their commanders, the men began to falter, then to fall back, and finally broke in a complete rout. General Howard boldly threw himself into the breach and attempted to rally the shattered columns; but his efforts were perfectly futile. The men were panic-stricken, and no power on earth could rally them in the face of the enemy. Information of the catastrophe was promptly communicated to General Sickles, who thus had a moment given him to prepare for the shock he instantly apprehended his column would suffer. With the coolness and skillfulness of a veteran of a hundred campaigns he set to work making his dispositions. The rebel forces were pressing hard upon the flying Germans, who could only escape by rushing across his lines, with every prospect of communicating the panic to them. It was a critical moment. But it did not stagger the citizen soldier. Calling to one after another of his staff, he sent them all off, one after another, lest any should fail in getting through, to warn Birney of his danger, and order him to fall back. Then, turning to General Pleasanton, he ordered him to take charge of the artillery, and turn it all upon the woods encircling the field, and support it with his cavalry. At the same moment large masses of the rebel infantry came dashing through the woods on the north and west close up to the field, and opened a tremendous fire of musketry into the confused mass of men and animals. To add to the confusion and terror of the scene night was rapidly approaching.

May I never be a witness to another such scene!

General Sickles, the New York politician, always got an extremely good press, for no reason discoverable at this late date.

It was about the same time that the other weekly, *Leslie's*, began publishing a series of what may be called emotional moments, the soap opera of the day.

We publish two portraits of one of the most gallant scouts in our army — J. W.

The midnight interview

The scout Davidson on duty *(left)*; off duty *(right)*

Davidson of the Eleventh Army Corps. He is a native of New York, and on the outbreak of the rebellion raised the Star-Spangled Banner on Trinity and St. Paul's Churches in this city. He accompanied General Burnside to North Carolina, and on the capture of Newbern raised the Stars and Stripes on the steeple of Christ's Church in that city, in view of the flying rebels. Mr. Davidson is a sailor by trade, and as might be supposed from his calling, is a man of cool head, quick eye, and solid nerve. In manners he is gentle and unassuming.

In the Civil War the terms "scout" and "spy" were indistinguishable and interchangeable. It is highly probable that Mr. Davidson at one time or another had served behind the rebel lines, as most scouts did, and that the publicity given him here, the reason for which is not discoverable, was in the nature of an announcement that he was going to stick to scouting.

At this period, in the middle of 1863, the scouting and intelligence service of the Army of the Potomac was distinctly bad. When Hooker turned north after Lee in the Gettysburg campaign, he kept pestering Washington for information about the enemy's strength and whereabouts, but the War Department was forced to reply that the only information they had was coming from his own contact reports.

Matters did not impove until Sheridan came east. In the west Sheridan had worked with Grenville M. Dodge, who was not only a good officer at obtaining contact information but also an extremely adroit employer of spies. As chief of cavalry, Sheridan naturally fell heir to the information service job, and he instantly set up an espionage system of great effectiveness. The head of his Richmond line was the famous "Crazy Betty" Van Lew, who used to toddle about the streets in funny hats and talking to herself, but who deserves the designation of a master spy if anyone ever did.

About the time the public was digesting the news from Chancellors-

Headquarters of the Union Army commanded by General Grant, on the banks
of the Mississippi near Vicksburg

ville, tidings of quite another kind
began to come in. The first word was:

On the morning of 30th April, General
Sherman, with a fleet of transports, accompanied by gun-boats, passed up the
Yazoo and made an attack on the rebel
batteries. In the afternoon several more
transports followed, with troops on board.
It is reported that General Sherman landed
precisely in the same place he did when
he made the former attack. Cannonading
and musketry were distinctly heard at
Young's Point that day, till long after
nightfall.

Then comes:

The railroad between Vicksburg and
Jackson has been cut by our cavalry, and
another attack upon that strong-hold has
been commenced. General Sherman has
landed a force in the Yazoo, near the point

where he landed before, and General
Grant has disembarked his army on the
Mississippi side of the river a few miles
below Vicksburg.

The cutting of the railroad was by
Grierson's cavalry raid through the
state, all the way to Baton Rouge.
But the rather odd thing to us today
is that the whole Grant movement
was treated as one of minor importance
and only given the same space accorded to a minor engagement in
Arkansas and the capture of a celebrated blockade runner. No one realized that after months of toiling
through the swamps, digging canals,
and trying other devices, Grant had
at last reached the high ground on the
east bank of the river and was off on
one of the boldest and most decisive
campaigns of history.

Attack of the gunboats on Grand Gulf

The fact is that no one understood what was going on, and most especially Pemberton, the Confederate commander, did not.

The following week comes an account of Porters ironclads battering the works at Grand Gulf, below Vicksburg, and then:

On Saturday we reached Port Gibson and took formal possession of the town. Just as we entered the village we discovered the suspension bridge which crosses the Bayou Pierre on fire. This compelled us to remain a few hours, while a floating bridge was constructed. The enemy appeared on the opposite side of the bayou, above and below the town, and shots were exchanged, but with no damage to our army.

Port Gibson is well inland, to the northeast of Grant's landing, but still people did not understand what was happening. Neither did Pemberton; he was feeling for Grant's nonexistent communications.

There was an almost anxious willingness not to be too excited about the news from Grant. Everybody knew that Pemberton had a large army in Vicksburg and Joe Johnston another one in central Mississippi. But now came more news:

The capture of Jackson, the capital of Mississippi, by the Union army of General Grant is now fully confirmed by the admission of Vicksburg and Jackson papers, and by dispatches from Mobile and Chattanooga. General Hurlbut telegraphs from Cairo to General Halleck that the fact is stated by the above authorities. The rebel General Gregg abandoned Raymond on Tuesday the 12th. On the next day he was reinforced by General Walker, of Georgia, at Mississippi Springs; but their combined forces were driven

Destruction of Rebel property at Jackson, Mississippi, May 15

The Battle of Raymond. Rebel charge on Logan's division

back to Jackson on Thursday. Our troops then followed, and took possession of the city from the east.

It is worth noting that word of this success came from Confederate sources and not Grant. He had, in fact, wired Halleck: "You may not hear from me for several days," and was out of communication. This had its advantages, to be sure: when the horrified Halleck tried to recall Grant for doing something so unmilitary as abandoning his communications in enemy country, the message did not get through. But it deprived the Northern public of any news of that wonderful series of battles going off like a train of explosions — Raymond, Jackson, Champion Hill, the Big Black — in which Grant chipped part after part off Pemberton's army and flung the defeated remnant into Vicksburg.

The artists were with the army, but their pictures did not reach the weeklies until nearly a month after the event, and then it was overlaid by

Skirmishing in the woods on the advance to Vicksburg

the news of Lee's Northward movement, the siege of Vicksburg itself and Grant's attempts to storm the place. This is typical:

Vicksburg had not been taken at 9 A.M. on 22d, but our men completely encircled the town, their colors were planted on a portion of the rebel works, and the gun and mortar-boats were at work in front. It is understood that General Grant intercepted a dispatch from Jeff Davis to General Pemberton promising him 100,000 men by way of reinforcements if he would hold out for two weeks. We have some rumors from rebel sources by way of Fortress Monroe; but they are so contradictory, if not purposely confused, that little can be made of them. Stories were afloat in this city on 27th, evidently echoes of rebel reports, that General Grant had been three times repulsed by Pemberton on 22d. Our advices are to a later hour on the evening of that day, but they make no mention of repulse.

This was the first dispatch after the one announcing the capture but not the battle of Jackson. It is not so much that the reporting was bad as that there was hardly any reporting at all; the lines of communication were out.

It is probably for this reason that hardly anyone realized at the time just what Grant had accomplished and was accomplishing. It took military men long after the war to find out; contemporaries never thought of him as a general who moved fast, kept the enemy off balance, and deceived him.

Once the siege of Vicksburg was established, correspondents and artists swarmed around the place, and the reporting became considerably more detailed. It was a much more active seige than one usually thinks of today. The rumors about Grant making an assault on May 22 and being repulsed turned out to be perfectly true; he lost 4000 men.

The forged letter

Fort Hill was a high salient on the north side of the city, with a slow stream making a natural moat around most of its base. Sherman commanded for the Union here, and some of his men being miners from the north country, he determined to mine the place out. Galleries were driven under the hill, and on June 25 a ton of powder was exploded, an event which greatly interested the artist-correspondents. Nothing much came of it; the assaulting party that rushed forward into the crater could go no farther, and the men were ultimately driven out by hand grenades. At almost the same time the ironclad *Cincinnati,* which had tried to close in and enfilade the place from the river, was sunk by plunging fire from the heights.

This was not enough to make Sherman give up his mining, however. He had another gallery driven in the Fort Hill sector, and on July 1 touched off a second ton of powder. This time he blew a bastion into the air with about 25 of its inhabitants, but no attempt was made to follow

115

The siege of Vicksburg. *Above:* Scene at General Logan's headquarters, June 25. *Middle:* Cannon dismounted inside the Rebel works (sketched with a glass from the rifle pits). *Below:* The 23rd Indiana and 45th Illinois, Leggett's brigade, Logan's division, M'Pherson's corps, storming Fort Hill after the explosion of the mine, June 26

The seige of Vicksburg. Approach of M'Pherson's saps to the Rebel works

it up with an assault, in view of what happened the first time. The effort of the besiegers was constantly to close in on and restrict the defense, wearing it down and tiring it out.

Our outer line is within one hundred yards of the rebel works. Our sharpshooters prevent the rebels from working their guns. The rebel works in the rear of the city are far more formidable than those in front. General Joe Johnston is in the neighborhood of Jackson with about fifteen thousand men, and is reported to be short of provisions and ammunition. General Grant has taken 8400 prisoners and 84 pieces of artillery.

The weeklies, at least, never got a hint of Grant's difficulty with General McClernand, which led to that vainglorious officer being sent home. They were a good deal more concerned with what went on in the trenches and the zigzag saps that were gradually carried forward toward the Confederate lines.

Davis, the artist who did the siege picture, describes his own work:

The siege of Vicksburg. Explosion of Hickenloper's mine under the Rebel Fort Hill

The seige of Vicksburg. Sharpshooters in the rifle pits constructed by Captain Hickenloper

118

Each hour's labor of our gallant men makes such a change in the scene that it must be a busy pencil that keeps before the readers of *Harper's Weekly* the workings of this regular siege.

Certainly it is very hot, but our men work steadily, and with a comprehension of plan that is surprising. But to the description of the scene sketched. In the center of the sketch and directly over our advanced battery, is the "rebel" work Fort Hill; still over this, and in the distance, Vicksburg is seen; too, in the distance, rises the smoke of our transports and gunboats, marking the course of the great river for whose uninterrupted navigation this mighty labor is progressing.

The trench or sap is at the moment just under the corner of the rebel work.

To-morrow will see another sap.

An oddity of the siege was the use of homemade mortars, produced by boring out hard logs and shrinking iron bands around them. They did not last long or have much range, but there was no particular need for either.

The weekly, so ecstatic over the capture of Island No. 10 and Memphis, was considerably more restrained about the almost simultaneous news of the surrender of Vicksburg and the Battle of Gettysburg.

It is assumed by some of our papers and many of our people that the defeat of Lee's army and the fall of Vicksburg involve the collapse of the rebellion. This may be so in one sense, inasmuch as the reopening of the Mississippi which follows as a matter of course from the cap-

The seige of Vicksburg. General Grant meeting Rebel General Pemberton at the stone house inside the Rebel works, on the morning of July 4

*Above:* The surrender of Vicksburg. The Rebels marching out and stacking arms.

*Below:* The surrender of Vicksburg. View of the city from the river bank, showing part of the river batteries

ture of Vicksburg and the defeat of the rebel army render the further prosecution of the contest by the pro-slavery insurgents absolutely hopeless.

But it will probably prove a mistake to expect the actual surrender of the rebels, so long as Bragg, Beauregard and Johnston have armies under their control. A contest may be carried on for years which, though hopeless and ineffectual to produce any good result, may yet avail to prevent our being able to claim that the rebellion had been crushed or peace restored. This, we take it, will be the policy of the rebel leaders. They are not the kind of men who "give up." They will fight to the bitter end: fight so long as they can persuade a single deluded white man or wretched negro to shoulder a musket in their cause.

Not only restrained but rather remarkably accurate as an estimate.

The picture of the actual surrender has a curious feature: both generals are in civilian clothes. The artist was probably perfectly right, but one wonders why.

On the evening of June 8 two officers rode into the camp of the 78th Illinois, of Rosecrans' army. They said they were Colonel Austin and Major Dunlap of the Inspector-General's department and exhibited orders to prove it, had dinner with Colonel Baird of the Illinois regiment, and, borrowing $50 from him on a note of hand, started toward Nashville.

After they had left, it occurred to Baird that there was something very odd about these two guests. Officers of the Inspector-General's department ordinarily come from, not go to, the

Execution by hanging of two Rebel spies, Williams and Peters, in the Army of the Cumberland, June 9, 1863

121

Capture of the Rebel ironclad *Atlanta* by the monitor *Weehawken*, Captain Rodgers

rear areas of the army; they had shown no interest in doing any inspecting; and why should men as far up the line in rank suddenly find themselves without money? Baird sent a group of cavalry to bring them back and did a little questioning. The answers were vague and then evasive; he placed them under arrest and wired Rosecrans' headquarters, where they would know. The answer was that Rosecrans knew nothing of any such persons, and the orders bearing his signature must be forged.

This touched off a search, in the course of which "Major Dunlap's" sword was drawn from his scabbard

In the toils of the siren

and found to be engraved: *Lt. W. G. Peters, C.S.A.* That wrapped it up; Baird had them tried by drumhead court-martial and hanged the next morning after they had confessed.

On June 17 a new Confederate ironclad, *Atlanta,* poked her prow out of Wasaw Sound and headed toward the monitors *Weehawken* and *Nahant,* which were blockading the place. Behind her was a little parade of excursion boats to watch the fun.

These were two of the new monitors, armed with one 15-inch gun and one 100-pound rifle each, and now permitted for the first time to use full powder charges. The resulting battle was something of a fiasco. *Atlanta* fired three times without getting any hits. *Weehawkens'* first shot was a 15-inch that went right through the Confederate ship's armor, wounding 16 men and knocking 40 more to the deck. A 100-pounder smashed a port shutter and wounded 17 more men; then came another 15-inch, which demolished the pilothouse, wounded the two pilots, and laid the quartermasters on the deck. Another 100-pounder had just gone through *Atlanta's* funnel when her captain hauled down her flag and replaced it with a white one.

The fact is that there was something queer about the Confederate ironclads, not even adequately explained by the shortage of materials, though that was a feature. After the first one, *Virginia*, they became steadily less powerful, less well armed, less protected, while the monitors as steadily improved in all three directions. Perhaps it was a shortage of competent dockyard labor.

Artists from the Vicksburg front were beginning to make people familiar with the Grant of later history; but through that June of 1863 the big news was the northward movement of Lee's army:

The prediction of the Richmond papers that the summer campaign would be fought on Northern soil was no idle threat. For some time past General Stuart has been massing the advance-guard of the rebel army near Culpepper, and on 9th a bloody fight took place between that body and a picked detachment of the Army of the Potomac. Of the results of this encounter we know nothing as yet. But unless Stuart has been utterly overwhelmed and scattered, we may take it for granted that even if our side has been successful the invasion of Pennsylvania has only been deferred for a time. The rebels are determined to make us feel "the horrors of war" in our homes. They are daring and desperate; there is every reason to expect, and no good reason to doubt, but that the soil of Pennsylvania and Maryland will be invaded within the month.

It may be asked, as it was asked when Lee invaded Maryland last fall, *cui bono?* What can the rebels gain by invading the North? They can gain simply this — that they will make our people feel the horrors of war, and give a practical point to the Copperhead cry for peace. They will both satisfy their thirst for vengeance and supply the citizens of Maryland and Pennsylvania with pretty substantial grounds for desiring the war to be ended. These ends, in the opinion of the Richmond press, amply justify the enterprise.

What are the prospects of success? The answer to this depends upon the Government at Washington. Because a brigade of swift cavalry was able to ride through the thinly-populated State of Mississippi without meeting any rebel force, that is no reason why a rebel *corps d'armee* should succeed in making good a foothold in the thickly-populated State of Pennsylvania—unless we are to suppose that the Government neglects the most obvious precautions for the protection of the North.

There is more of it, about "taking proper measures" of a kind unspecified and calling out the Pennsylvania militia, but this gives the essential picture of how reasonably calm thinking went at the time. In the light of what we know now, it has a remarkable gap—

Major General Ulysses S. Grant
("Unconditional Surrender")

the question of supply. It was shortage of supplies, particularly of shoes, that as much as anything else led Lee to make the invasion, though the prospect of applying moral pressure by a victory on Northern soil was never wholly absent. And the editorialist talked about a *"corps d'armee"* making good a foothold in Pennsylvania as though it would never run out of bullets, or could obtain them from the countryside on the same terms as food.

This is not surprising; there was an equal incomprehension of Grant's question of supply in the Vicksburg campaign. But it points up what one

The invasion of the North. Street scenes in Philadelphia

John Burns, the only man in Gettysburg, Pennsylvania, who fought at the battle

needs to look for in considering any military campaign.

It is also worth noting that the invasion had not actually taken place when this was written, but nobody had any doubt about what Lee was going to do.

John Burns, "Farmer" Burns, attained a certain temporal celebrity by showing up for the Battle of Gettysburg with his old rifle and the uniform he had worn in the War of 1812. Fell into line and fought all three days, too, and received no little publicity from it, which he studiously disregarded.

The weeklies made no effort to compete with the dailies in reporting the battle, as they did with Vicksburg. The story consisted of General Meade's dispatch of eight-thirty on the evening of July 3, when the issue had been decided (a curious note for modern readers is that only readers in the big cities, and not all of them, knew until well after the battle that it had been fought under Meade and not Hooker) Meade's order of congratulation to the army, and Lincoln's July 4 announcement to the nation:

The President announces to the country that the news from the Army of the Potomac up to ten P.M. of the 3d is such as to cover that army with the highest honor, to promise a great success to the cause of the Union, and to claim the condolence of all for the many gallant fallen; and that for this he especially desires that, on

*Above:* The Battle of Gettysburg. Hill on the left of the Union position. Hazlitt's battery in action. *Below:* The only contemporary drawing of Pickett's charge

The Battle of Gettysburg. Longstreet's attack upon our left center. Blue Ridge in the distance

this day, He, whose will, not ours, should ever be done, be every where remembered and reverenced with the profoundest gratitude.

Editorially, there was a little eagle-screaming and one would gather the opinion that the Army of Northern Virginia was very nearly destroyed, which turned out to be pretty far from the case. But what most especially interested the editors was not so much that a great battle had been fought and won as a mass meeting in New York:

And on this day a body of people who call themselves "the Democracy" held a mass meeting in the Academy of Music, under the auspices of a political society known as the Democratic Young Men's Association, which is the Copperhead club before which Vallandigham, James Brooks, G. Ticknor Curtis, and their associates, have furiously denounced the war, or craftily undermined public confidence in the national cause. The building was filled. The crowd was enthusiastic, after the manner of crowds on the Fourth. The speakers were chiefly Governor Seymour of New York, and Mr. Seymour, who is not Governor of Connecticut. They made long and emphatic harangues. The New York Seymour, who says he will let the

Auld Lang Syne courtship renewed

128

Union go rather than slavery, complained that we give a dull assent to the doctrine of human equality set forth in the Declaration, and therefore we ought to let men who rebel in arms to perpetuate slavery have their own way. He informed us that our national authorities are despots and tyrants; that the fundamental principles of our Government, all our securities, all our rights are in mortal danger from — the Government of the United States. Mr. Seymour of Connecticut said, as usual, that we are beaten; and even if we were not, we could not hope to beat a gallant race of gentlemen who whip the mothers of their infants and sell their own children. We must make peace by asking them what they wanted, and doing precisely what they said.

The pictorial coverage of Gettysburg did not begin until July 25, except for a few portraits of Meade and Reynolds; and even then was not very good. The artists seem to have been well behind the army.

Even though drawn after the event, the picture on page 127 — which is of the attack on Sickles' Corps on the second day of the battle — is somewhat better than most and demonstrates that the artists were learning something of what a battle really looks like.

But before the picture even appeared, another event supervened which carried the focus of interest temporarily from the war. It is worth remarking that this was very rare. The weeklies gave editorial coverage to Congress, and occasional pictorial and editorial coverage to such events as the visit of a Russian squadron or the new fashions from Paris; but the war remained the great focus of interest. With the draft riots it was different; they were not only war news in a sense, but they took place practically on the editorial doorstep. First report:

A fearful riot commenced in this city on the morning of Monday, July 13. At first it was merely a demonstration against the draft, which had been commenced on

Process of drafting in the 6th District in New York, August 19

Saturday in the Ninth District. The drawing of names was here resumed on Monday morning. A crowd, gradually increasing, gathered around the office, but the drawing went on until about 60 additional names had been drawn, when a sudden attack was made by the mob. The wheel was destroyed, the papers scattered, and the building set on fire. The excitement spread through the city; crowds assembled every where, at first with no apparent common object. But in a short time the aim of the leaders in the riot movement appeared to be an indiscriminate attack upon the colored people, and upon those who are supposed to be in any way connected with the draft or with the Republican party. Several buildings were sacked and burned. The *Tribune* office was attacked, and only saved by the vigorous efforts of the police; negroes were hunted down, several were murdered under the most revolting circumstances. The house of the Mayor was sacked, that of the Postmaster burned to the ground; railroad tracks were torn up, and for a while it seemed that the city was under control of the mob. The most dastardly performance was the destruction of the Colored Orphan Asylum, in which some hundreds of children were provided for. This was sacked, and finally burned to the ground. The riot raged throughout the whole of Monday and Tuesday. The movement, which was at first one of opposition to the draft, has developed into a scheme of plunder and robbery. As we write on Wednesday noon, it appears that the riot is quelled. It is too early to give the results, or to speak of the conduct of the public authorities.

This is pretty good reporting for someone writing while the riots were, in fact, still in progress. The editorial comment a week later deplores the fact that "grape and canister" were not used on the rioters early in the game; attributes the riots to "pernicious teachings widely scattered among the ignorant"; attempts to rebut the charge that most of the rioters were Irish; deplores the fact that only 80 men turned out in response to a call for volunteers; and comments that it would have a bad effect to send men from New Jersey or Pennsylvania to put down a riot in New York. A somewhat rambling editorial, in which a curious point is the failure to mention Governor Seymour's "pernicious teachings" by direct attribution.

It takes a little analysis to understand why the draft produced such a strong reaction in the North while the earlier Confederate conscription act met no such resistance. The facts are clear; after the New York draft riots a dozen cities—Buffalo, Elmira, Oswego, Chicago, Peoria, Iowa City, and others — asked for postponement or abandonment of the draft, and practically every governor in the North asked for some special privilege in

129

Draft riots in New York. Exciting

scenes during the Reign of Terror

The Army of the Potomac. Drawing rations

connection with it. These ranged from Missouri, which wished its drafted men assigned to serve under German commanders only, to New Hampshire, which demanded that its draftees be supplied with the best modern rifles only, and Rhode Island, which wanted its drafted men to be made into a special corps to protect the coast against Confederate privateers. In short, there was general opposition.

In part this was a fear reaction due to the fact that the New York riots fortuitously took place at the very beginning of the process and other authorities anticipated the same kind of trouble. Philadelphia, for example, asked for troops to enforce the draft. But there was also a deeper reason, and it lay in the system by which the Northern armies had been recruited from the beginning. They were volunteer organizations, which commonly elected their own minor officers, while the colonels were appointed by the governors.

The governors were so extremely loath to give up this source of patronage that the repeated efforts to have old regiments recruited up to strength broke down on the fact that it was easier to make new regiments with new colonels. There was continual pressure on the War Department to permit the formation of six- and even three-month state regiments, especially of cavalry, with arms, mounts, and pay being furnished by Washington. Andrew Johnson of Tennessee was a particular offender in this regard.

The draft thus represented the end of a sweet racket. The drafted men would pass out of control of state governments and into the general pool of national troops. The oddity is to see the Northern governors contending so vigorously for the states' rights doctrine they were fighting against.

Meanwhile the Army of the Potomac was doing nothing in large quantities and had time to examine camp life. A volunteer named Lawrence Van Alstyne set down his impression of the rations thus:

The camp kettles are large sheet-iron pails, one larger than the other so one can be put inside the other when moving. If we have meat and potatoes, meat is put into one and potatoes in the other. The one that gets cooked first is emptied into mess pans, which are large sheet-iron pans with flaring sides, so one can be packed in another. Then the coffee is put in the empty kettle and boiled. The bread is cut into thick slices and the breakfast call sounds. We grab our plates and cups and wait for no second invitation. We each get a piece of meat and a potato, a chunk of bread and a cup of coffee with a spoonful of brown sugar in it. Milk and butter we buy, or go without. We save a piece of bread for the last, with which we wipe up everything and then eat the dish rag. Dinner and breakfast are alike, only sometimes the meat and potatoes are cut up and cooked together, which makes a delicious stew. The cooks are men detailed from the ranks for that purpose. I never yet saw the cooks wash their hands, but presume they do when they go to the brook for water.

From other sources we learn that the meat was usually salt pork, rarely ham or bacon, with salt beef and fresh meat ranking as delicacies. The bread was most commonly hardtack, a flour-and-water biscuit guaranteed to exercise the teeth. The standard ration was 12 ounces of pork or 20 ounces of beef per day, pork being considered more nourishing than beef for no discoverable reason. Beans and peas appeared rarely, and usually in the dried form; they were a nuisance to cook. Potatoes usually disappeared when an army was on the march, as they took up a good deal of transportation. White sugar was still a citified delicacy, and molasses often replaced even the brown sugar.

Few events in the war excited more indignation in the North than the attack on Lawrence, Kansas, the old center of free state sentiment in that state. Contemporary account:

The city of Lawrence was, on the evening of August 20, 1863, one of the most thriving towns between the Missouri River and the Rocky Mountains. At daybreak on the next day it was a heap of ruins. A gang

The war in Kansas. Fearful massacre at Lawrence by Quantrell's guerrillas.

and the house burned over their bodies. The number of victims is stated at 180, including the Mayor and the principal citizens. Only one hotel was left standing, and this was spared because the guerrilla chief had been formerly entertained there free of expense. Two of the banks were plundered, and the third escaped because the marauders could not force the safe in time. The total loss of property is put down at two millions of dollars. No other such instance of wanton brutality has occurred during the war.

As a matter of fact this was an understatement. Lawrence had been practically wiped out, with 205 men killed, many more badly hurt, and 182 buildings burned, with hardly anything of value left in the town.

The unappreciated point, at the time, was that Quantrell held no commission from the Confederacy nor any state in it, and most of his men were deserters from the Confederate Army or simply frontier desperadoes. Two of them, in fact, were Frank and Jesse James; that was how these romantic characters got their start. The whole affair—and it was not the only one of its kind—was simply a product of chaotic frontier conditions during the war. Kansas had a strong element from the South, men quite willing to help anyone who bore down hard on abolitionists, even though the method was not too nice. As a result Quantrell could count on support from part of the population and got it. But his operation was self-destructive; his band included a considerable number of those individuals who, having made a haul, wanted to settle down on the proceeds, and many of them did so.

The big news of the late summer of 1863 was the attack on Charleston, regarded in the North as the major focus of the rebellion, second in importance only to Richmond. The place was not only intrinsically important; the war in other theaters was for the

of guerrillas, 800 strong, under Quantrell, crossed the Missouri River on the evening of the 20th, and pushed forward to Lawrence, where they arrived just before daybreak. Guards were posted around the town so as to prevent all escape, and the work of pillage and murder at once commenced. The attack was wholly unexpected, and there was not the least show of resistance. The citizens were massacred in the light of their burning homes, and their bodies flung into wells and cisterns. In one case twelve men were driven into a building, where they were shot down,

*Above:* Bombardment of Fort Wagner, Charleston, South Carolina. *Below:* Union sharpshooters in front of Fort Wagner, Charleston, South Carolina

135

The siege of Charleston. Attack on Battery Gregg, September 5, 1863

moment not very newsworthy, with Meade facing Lee inactively in Virginia, Rosecrans maneuvering obscurely against Bragg in the pine-barren country of Tennessee, and most of Grant's army distributed after the capture of Vicksburg.

The expedition was under Admiral John A. Dahlgren, with a cooperating force of troops under General Q. A. Gilmore. DuPont had tried to take the place by hammering straight into the harbor; Dahlgren and Gilmore tried to reduce it by inches, first attacking Morris Island at the southern entrance to the harbor. Near the northern end of this island was a regularly bastioned fort, Fort Wagner; on the very tip was an outlying battery, Battery Gregg.

Dahlgren had the eight monitors and the big broadside ironclad *New Ironsides*, which saw more fighting than any ship in American history. The siege, which has found little place in history because it was isolated and inconclusive, began on the night of July 7, with Gilmore landing on the southern tip of Morris Island. Next morning an assault was tried under the cover of four monitors. It failed, and operations settled down into a

steady siege, the ironclads moving in every day to shell Wagner and fight off the batteries of Fort Moultrie on the northern side of the entrance and the island fortress of Fort Sumter.

*Harper's* artist was on the monitor *Catskill* a good deal of the time. He reported on one occasion that the ship had been hit 60 times in the course of a single day of firing, and this was not uncommon, but Dahlgren had learned at what distance to place his monitors so that their armor would not be penetrated. Still it was heavy work in the heat, and occasionally a shot from the forts would find a port or pilothouse. Officer after officer became so ill he had to be sent home.

The reporting of the long siege, which lasted all through July and August, was mostly pictorial, since there was very little of event to chronicle. About the only event of the siege was:

At midnight on the 19th a large iron side-wheel steamer, having escaped the fire of the guns of the outside blockading fleet, was just crossing the bar when Captain Rodgers (*of Catskill*) arrested her progress by two shots from our 11 and 15 inch guns. The vessel ran ashore near Sullivan's Island, and became a total wreck— a warning to all Anglo-Rebels to keep away from Charleston during the present siege.

During the siege Gilmore succeeded in setting up a heavy gun in the swamps at the rear of Morris Island itself. This was the "Swamp Angel"; it could reach Charleston itself and caused intense indignation, the Confederate press comparing "Monster" Gilmore with "Beast" Butler and vowing he should be hanged when caught, something of which few echoes survive.

On the night of September 5 a boat attack on Battery Gregg was tried. It did not succeed, but the next day the Confederate chief of engineers reported Wagner as untenable, and under cover of darkness it was evacuated.

Gilmore now installed his own batteries on the island, and with the monitors moving into the harbor to assist, began shelling Fort Sumter. The place was soon reduced to a heap of rubble, but a night boat attack on it failed. Dahlgren called a council of war, after which he reported to Washington that there were still five lines of obstructions and torpedoes before he could close in on the batteries that had been erected close to the city itself. He estimated that he would lose five monitors breaking through, but if the Department would send him that many more, he would try.

This was, of course, too much for Washington, and the siege was abandoned. None of this appears in the contemporary press; the subject of Charleston was simply quietly dropped, there was no more news from the place and other events seemed more important.

One of Lincoln's chief anxieties during the early part of the war was for the loyalists of East Tennessee, of whom Parson Brownlow was a representative. He constantly urged the War Department to do something for them, and by September of 1863 the draft had brought in enough new men so that it was possible to send General

The siege of Charleston. The "swamp angel" opening on Charleston

The siege of Charleston. The last night before Wagner. The head of the sap

Burnside, with a new Army of the Ohio, through Cumberland Gap to Knoxville.

Contemporary reporting of the event may be described as restrained. It consisted chiefly of reproductions of the official dispatches, and as there was no action to chronicle, these were neither very long nor very detailed.

Meanwhile the Army of the Potomac maintained its condition of stasis facing Lee in Virginia, and the coverage came down to scenes and incidents of camp life. Those opposite are typical.

Since General Meade has been in command a marked change has been apparent in head-quarter arrangements. All the cover now carried by officers against the

weather is a few tent flies, which are pitched like a small gable roof, as seen in the sketch, open on all sides. The wagon train is left in the rear, and a few light vehicles and ambulances, to carry the necessary blankets and frugal supplies of the officers, is all that accompanies the staff. The drawing represents the local habitation of the medical director, Dr. Letterman, who in company with the Surgeon-General, Dr. De Boyse, and Dr. Davis, are to be seen taking soup on the ground by the fly. The camp is in a fine grove of oaks.

That is, the Army of the Potomac was substantially on vacation, and there was something in Lincoln's remark to Meade that if he could not move against Lee with a three-to-two

The Army of Potomac. *Above:* Sharpshooter improvising a rest for his rifle. *Below:* The Bedouin tent

superiority, Lee would be in the same position and the troops had better be used somewhere else.

No international incident of the war; not even the Trent affair, received more contemporary attention than the construction of the two "Laird Rams" for the Confederacy in England. We know today that after Ambassador Charles Francis Adams' remark that: "It is idle to point out to your lordship that this is war," they were never delivered, but the outcome was not visible then, and the press was considerably exercised.

The picture of Laird's Anglo-Rebel rams is from a drawing obtained by some patriotic citizens who were lately in England.

They smuggled an artist into the yard in which the unscrupulous knave, Laird, is building his pirates, and succeeded in getting a pretty thorough picture.

There follows an eyewitness description of the launch of one of the rams, and then a description of the vessels themselves, which contain some remarkable details:

There are two turrets or towers, about twenty feet in diameter and ten in height. They are placed partly above and below decks; are pierced for two heavy guns each, entered below decks through six man-holes; they are built of very heavy boiler-iron on the outside and inside, and to be filled in with a foot's thickness of wool or some more resisting material. They revolve on twenty-four wheels (similar to

General Burnside's army occupying Cumberland Gap

The Anglo-Rebel pirates. Steam ram building for the Rebels in the Clyde, Scotland

the small wheels of a locomotive, radiating from a centre) on axles of wrought iron, to the circle of the diameter of the turrets. The top of the turrets (and deck) is protected by thick iron. Each vessel has a powerful engine, of between 300 and 400 horsepower.

The artist-observer did a good job; the ships looked pretty much as represented. But he picked up his description from a poor source; the boiler-iron-and-wool armor not only never existed; it was fantastic.

The Anglo-Rebel pirates. One of Laird's steam rams

Service and shoddy. A picture of the times

The artist and his model

The war on the Mississippi. Secesh ladies coming to the United States commissaries for provisions

The Siege of Charleston. *Above:* The Segar steamer which propelled the Rebel torpedo. *Below:* Attempt to blow up *Ironsides* by a Rebel torpedo

On the night of October 5, 1863, submarine warfare began with an attack on *New Ironsides,* off Charleston. The watch saw something like a cigar coming toward her, hailed, and was answered by a charge from a shotgun, which killed the officer of the deck. The next moment the ship was laid nearly on her beam-ends by the explosion of a torpedo which had been carried on a spar projecting from the semisubmerged craft. The ironclad did not sink and her return fire destroyed the torpedo craft, which took down the two men who were below, handling the engines. The other pair, Glasell and Toombs, were captured; they gave descriptions of their "nondescript" (as it was called in contemporary reports) and from these descriptions the weekly's artist produced both a surprisingly accurate picture and a good account of the event.

On September 19, 1863, Lincoln was awakened from sleep to be handed a telegram from Charles A. Dana, the War Department's special seeing eye with Rosecrans' Army of the Cumberland:

My report today is of deplorable importance. Chickamauga is as fatal a name in our history as Bull Run. Van Cleve on

The Battle of Chickamauga. Thomas' men repulsing the charges of the Rebels

Thomas' right was seen to give way, but in tolerable order, borne down by immense columns of the enemy. Before them our soldiers turned and fled. It was a wholesale panic. We have lost heavily in killed today. The total of our killed, wounded and prisoners can hardly be less than 20,000 and may be much more.

The papers had most of it by morning and some of them printed it under turn rules, while Lincoln paced the floor, unable to sleep. But as the day developed, it began to appear that all the returns were not in. Dana telegraphed that his earlier dispatch may have "given too dark a view of the situation," and correspondents who were allowed to send dispatches from Chattanooga became more cheerful.

Still it was almost a week before the full story of Chickamauga began to come out, and even then there was no appreciation of the fact that the rout of the Union right and center had been produced by a mistaken order from Rosecrans which left a wide gap in the Union line. Nevertheless, there was complete and immediate appreciation of the key event of the battle: the tremendous stand made by Thomas at Horseshoe Ridge after two thirds of the army had been driven from the field.

Pictures of him, generally inaccurate, began to appear in the weeklies, together with drawings of the battle. The one given here is typical and is probably an eyewitness job; this was one occasion where the men were in close order.

Yet even so, there was incomplete appreciation of what Thomas had accomplished by holding firm on the ridge, riding along the lines and turning back the last attacks with the bayonet when there were no more bullets, while Rosecrans, swept away to Chattanooga in the tide of fugitives, was wiring to have Cincinnati and Louisville placed in a state of defense.

The war in Georgia. Arrival at Stevenson, Alabama, of the wounded from the battlefield of Chickamauga, September 23

"You have conquered, I am here!"

For it was not merely Bragg that Thomas turned back at Chickamauga; it was Bragg plus Longstreet's whole corps from the invincible Army of Northern Virginia.

The event was fatal. After the war, D. H. Hill, one of the more thoughtful Southern generals, put the matter: "After Chickamauga the élan of the Southern soldier was never seen again. He fought stoutly to the last, but after Chickamauga with the sullenness of despair and without enthusiasm or hope." Before that battle it had always been possible to explain defeats, when they occurred, as due to superior Union numbers or equipment, and they were so explained. Chickamauga was another story. It was fought on Southern ground, with a not inconsiderable superiority of numbers on the Confederate side, their best generals and best troops — and that Southern soldier of whom D. H. Hill speaks realized, even if the newspapers behind him did not, that the victory was purely tactical and technical. They had failed to destroy or even seriously shake Thomas; and before such resolution their own began to give way.

There was also the point that Chattanooga, the gate of the mountains, was the main object of the campaign, and Chickamauga did no more than install Rosecrans in it. This fact, at least, was appreciated at the time. Says the weekly:

The Richmond *Dispatch*, commenting on the late battle in Georgia, puts the rebel Iliad in a nut-shell. "Unless, however,

Rosecrans be driven across the river, our late victory will have been of no value."

This is the truth concisely told. For what, in that case, will have been gained to the rebel cause by Bragg's advantage? Some guns—nothing more. There has been a battle. The loss on both sides is great. The armies withdraw. If, then, there is no reoccupation of territory, the only question is which of the combatants could best afford to lose men. How many such battles could the rebels safely fight? In the condition to which they have been reduced a barren victory is necessarily a disaster. Consequently although Bragg claimed a "complete victory" and "a route" of the enemy, the wiser rebels, who have been disciplined by the dispatches of Beauregard, declared that they waited to see Chattanooga retaken before they gave way to joy.

Should any disaster befall Burnside or Rosecrans be compelled to abandon Chattanooga and retire northward, the rebels may justly claim a decided advantage. Anything short of this is a disaster for them. Bunker Hill never ranked high among British victories, although the Americans withdrew.

At this period of 1863 Secretary of State Seward became agitated, perhaps correctly so, over the fact that Napoleon III's troops had set up an empire for Maximilian in Mexico. It seemed to him probable that the French would either reclaim Texas for Mexico or support its independence, and he urged the seizure of some part of the state as a demonstration of sovereignty so strongly that the military people could not refuse, although they doubted the strategic wisdom of the step.

The attempt was made at Sabine Pass, the extreme eastern corner of the state, with 500 troops covered by the gunboats *Clifton, Sachem,* and *Arizona,* an ill-assorted squadron. All three were conversions, *Clifton* a ferryboat, *Sachem* a tug, *Arizona* an ocean steamer. The last could not get close enough to the fort to use her guns effectively. In trying to run past it to enfilade, *Sachem* was hit in the boiler, drifted ashore, and had to surrender. *Clifton,* in action for some time, ran aground, became a sitting target, lost her walking beam, and was also hit in the steam drum, so she had to give up, too.

The incident was reported accurately by a private in an Indiana regiment aboard one of the transports, with no attempt to call it anything but a dis-

The war in Texas. Disabling and capture of the Union gunboats *Sachem* and *Clifton* in the attack on Sabine Pass, Texas, September 8

Shaving in camp. A scene in General Meade's army near Culpepper

aster. It was given rather surprisingly large space in the weeklies and received good pictorial coverage from the same private.

After Chickamauga, Bragg detached Longstreet's corps to take Knoxville from Burnside. There was a good deal of confused skirmishing that had no name as battles; the Confederates had a good deal more cavalry and used it continually. This seems to have made Burnside somewhat excessively nervous, and it was probably fortunate that the War Department's Dana reached him just after the news that Longstreet was on the march. Dana reported:

I found him possessed of the idea that he must expose his whole force to capture rather than withdraw from the country.

General Wilson [he was one of Grant's staff officers] overcame it by representing that Grant did not wish him to include the capture of his entire army among the elements of his plan of operations.

Grant had been placed in charge of all the armies west of the mountains and Rosecrans removed, to be replaced by Thomas. Dana's report caused considerable anxiety in Washington; the right thing to do was visibly to remove Burnside also, but he had a good deal of influence, was highly popular, and it would have a poor effect to relieve him without some obvious reason.

Washington was therefore anxious and urged Grant to do something that would force Longstreet's recall to Bragg. None of this got into the press;

The war in Tennessee. Rebel cavalry attacking a United States supply train near Jasper, Tennessee

when East Tennessee was mentioned it was always in terms of how popular Burnside was and how well the Union troops were received.

The fighting at Chattanooga was extremely complicated and it is hardly surprising that the correspondents did not report well something they were very far from understanding. Yet there is a striking failure on the part of the correspondents to grasp, if not the whole of the situation, then its most important details.

For instance, the XI and XII Corps were taken from the Army of the Potomac and shipped to Chattanooga under Hooker by railroad. It was an achievement of the first order, since the journey was made in a single week; and it must be remembered that the railroads did not connect in most of the large cities, there were no bridges over the Ohio, and some of the rail lines involved had different gauges. It was not reported at all, even after the Chattanooga battles, when Hooker's men had made their presence decidedly obvious.

The next act was the establishment of the "Cracker Line" for the reprovisioning of Chattanooga, which had been substantially blockaded by Bragg, since the roads north of the city were so poor that only a barely sufficient amount of supply could be hauled over them. This drew some comment:

The evacuation of Lookout Mountain, some weeks since by order of General Rosecrans, gave to the rebels complete command of the river between this place and Bridgeport.

Lookout Mountain. The Rebels shelling our camps

The Army of the Cumberland. General Hazen's brigade descending the
Tennessee to occupy Lookout Valley

General Grant, in taking command,
found that the river could be opened to
within a short distance of this place; and
to accomplish this was his first work. A
portion of our forces crossed at Bridgeport, and came up the south bank of the
river. Other troops were sent at night to a
point on the north bank of the river below
the intended crossing-place.

The brigade of General Hazen was
placed in pontoons and floated at night to
a point below, and out of the range of the
rebel batteries upon Lookout Mountain,
where they arrived just before dawn. A
number of the boats landed at a point just
below the place where the bridge now is,
and at a rebel picket-station. The pickets
ran off, shouting *"Yanks! Yanks!! Yanks!!!"*
their pace being accelerated by a number
of musketballs from the before-mentioned
Yanks.

The building of the bridge was accomplished most successfully, though for some
time our men worked under a severe fire
from the rebel batteries.

The bridge is the best work of its kind
that has been constructed by the army at
this point, and was built by the Michigan
Engineers under the supervision of Captains Fox and Dresser.

This is good reporting as to the
incidents involved, but there is no
indication of what the bridge was for
or what was accomplished. The next

action was Hooker's advance into
Lookout Valley. This, too, was reported:

On the night of the 28th of October the
troops of General Hooker occupied a portion of Lookout Valley. Shortly after midnight it was discovered that the rebels had
occupied a strong post which placed our
troops in a very uncomfortable, if not untenable position. General Hooker at once
ordered the Thirty-third Massachusetts
and Seventy-third Ohio to storm and carry
the place with the bayonet. This they did
in the most gallant manner. In many places
the brave fellows had to drag themselves
up by grasping shrubs and roots.

When they reached the top the explosions of musketry burned the contending
troops. The captured rebels said it was a
disgrace to them that the place was taken,
but they could not help it; for, said they,
"you kept coming, and the next we knew
you were right among us."

Again this is all right as to the
details given, but there has been
omitted one of the most striking details
in the series of Chattanooga battles:
the fact that some mules stampeded,
and in the dark the Confederates mis-
took them for a charge of cavalry and
took to their heels. The correspondent
was evidently allowed to talk to some

of the prisoners, and surely there must have been one or two of them who at least mentioned the non-existent cavalry charge.

There was a good deal of reorganizational and supply work necessary and Grant wanted to wait for the arrival of Sherman's corps from the west before he began his attack. No hint of this or of the coming of Sherman appears. Instead this is the next item:

A dispatch from Chattanooga, of 10th instant, says that refugees from the rebel army report General Bragg to be evacuating his position in front of Chattanooga, and falling back to Rome or Atlanta. General Longstreet was said to be organizing a force for a raid on our line of communications at Bridgeport.

None of this was true at all — the purest rumor and moonshine. Bragg was staying right where he was, receiving a visit from Jefferson Davis, and Longstreet had Burnside under a loose kind of siege at Knoxville.

The next item is:

A dispatch from Atlanta, Georgia, says that a fight between the rebel batteries and our forces before Chattanooga continued briskly, and that our troops have made a diversion from right to left, with a view probably to attack Lookout Mountain, or, it may be, to send troops to reinforce General Burnside.

The Army of the Cumberland. Capture of Rebel rifle pits in Lookout Valley by the 33rd Massachusetts and 73rd Ohio Volunteers, on October 28, 1863

The Army of the Cumberland. General Baird's division capturing the Rebel guns on the left of Missionary Ridge

This is apparently the account of Sherman's movement, which was from right to left; it was not against Lookout Mountain but Missionary Ridge. It was accompanied by editorial opinion:

Our armies seem once more at a standstill. The November mud appears to have driven both Meade and Lee into winterquarters; and cavalry raids and outpost skirmishes are likely to be the only movements of consequence on the Potomac for some weeks to come. At Chattanooga all is quiet, and our correspondents write that no active operations are expected in that army for some time. Grant will have enough to do to hold and secure his communications, and feed his army at Chattanooga; while, on the other hand, Bragg will have his hands full in preparing for the inevitable movement on Atlanta and Rome.

Altogether the prospect is that our armies will not see much fighting, at all events, on this side of Christmas. With the early spring Meade may move, Grant is sure to move, and Gilmore may pursue his victorious career.

Grant was a good hand about keeping his own counsel on what he meant to do; but seldom has editorial judgment proved more wrong. Five days before this, Hooker had taken Lookout Mountain. Four days before, Grant struck and Bragg·was driven through the hills.

The event was announced in the weeklies in a dispatch from Grant saying he believed he was "not premature in announcing a complete victory over Bragg." It was accompanied by one from the army quartermaster claiming 6000 prisoners and 48 guns— which should have been the tip-off to editorial minds that something very unusual had taken place in northwest Georgia.

A later dispatch said Missionary Ridge was taken by surprise—the only mention of that incredible and heroic feat in which the Army of the Cum-

The rescue

berland ran away from its orders and went storming up the face of the mountain in the teeth of cannon and musketry to tear the rebel center to pieces.

That is, the verbal coverage of the battle was distinctly poor, distinctly sparse. The Army of the Potomac, sitting in its camps, received more space, and the grand ball given for the officers of a Russian squadron visiting New York a great deal more.

This was, no doubt, mainly the fault of the correspondents themselves. The data were there for them if they went after it. This is proved by the fact that the pictorial coverage of the Chattanooga actions was so extremely good. They missed hardly a thing, and even the night exploit of Hazen's brigade in gaining the foothold that opened the "Cracker Line" came from one of the artists. As to why the artists were so much better reporters than the reporters is a question not precisely easy to answer at this distant date. Perhaps it was because they could use the ampler space of the mails and were not limited by telegraph tolls.

*Leslie's* opened its description of the events of November 19 with a des-

The consecration of the Great National Cemetery near Gettysburg, Thursday,

cription of the place and the weather, and then went on:

The ceremonies began with a prayer by the Rev. Dr. Stockton, Chaplain of the House of Representatives. The Hon. Edward Everett then delivered his address, one of those classic, eloquent orations which have no equal in this country. Recalling the honors paid by Athens to her fallen brave, he spoke of the occasion which called them together, of the importance to all of the great battle, and what that victory effected. After glancing at the early history of the war, he gave an elaborate and highly-wrought account of the battle.

At the close President Lincoln addressed the assembly:

"Fourscore and seven years ago our fathers brought forth upon this continent a new nation, conceived in liberty and dedicated to the proposition that all men are created equal. Now we are engaged in a great civil war, testing the question whether this nation or any nation so conceived, so dedicated, can long endure. We are met on the great battlefield of that war. We are met to dedicate it, on a portion of the field set apart as the final restingplace of those who gave their lives for the nation's life; but the nation must live, and it is altogether fitting that we should do this.

"In a larger sense we cannot dedicate, we cannot consecrate, we cannot hallow this ground in reality. The number of men, living and dead, who struggled here have consecrated it far above our poor attempts to add to its consecration. The world will little know and nothing remember of what we see here, but we cannot forget what these brave men did here.

November 19, by President Abraham Lincoln, and his Cabinet

"We owe this offering to our dead. We imbibe increased devotion for that cause for which they here gave the last full measure of devotion; we here might resolve that they shall not have died in vain; that the nation shall, under God, have a new birth of freedom, and that the Government of the people, for the people, and for all people, shall not perish from earth."

There are some interesting textual variations from the accepted version that make one wonder where the magazine got its text of the speech. The other weekly did not print the text of the address, but had something to say about it editorially:

The President and the Cabinet were there, with famous soldiers and civilians. The oration by Mr. Everett was smooth and cold. Delivered, doubtless, with his accustomed graces, it yet wanted one stirring thought, one vivid picture, one thrilling appeal.

The few words of the President were from the heart to the heart. They can not be read, even, without kindling emotion. "The world will little note nor long remember what we say here, but it can never forget what they did here." It was as simple and felicitous and earnest a word as was ever spoken.

In other words, the editors knew very precisely at the time that Lincoln had made a great speech, a historic speech, even though Mr. Everett and Mr. Seward thought otherwise, and they took different methods of expressing their opinion. *Harper's* did not

give the event picture coverage; its Eastern artists seem to have been with the Army of the Potomac. Also, in spite of its salute to Lincoln for his speech, it was much more interested in the speech made by Henry Ward Beecher, who had just been given an enormous reception on his return from England. The leading editorial of the Gettysburg dedication week is a long disquisition on his experiences there, including some twisting of the lion's tail:

It is to avoid a rupture with this working population that Lord Palmerston has refused to recognize the rebels. He doubtless honestly expects to see the United States destroyed; and calculates that, when that cheerful catastrophe occurs, he will crush out democracy in England.

The war in Louisiana. The wreck of the gunboat *Cotton* in the Bayou Teche

The Confederate river gunboats were pretty much of a class. They were built around river tugs, usually stern- or side-wheelers. The normal procedure was to plank their sides with three or four inches of oak, install another oak bulkhead several inches inside, and fill the gap between the two with tightly pressed cotton, which for some reason was supposed to be especially resistant to shot. The bows were then shod with iron for ramming purposes.

There were about 20 of them altogether, and they never lived up to expectations, the principal reason being that both at New Orleans and Memphis the Union ships appeared with guns so heavy that the Confederate ships might as well not have been protected at all. After the spring of 1863 there was only one of the Confederate river ships left, keeping carefully out of sight up the Red River.

However this did not mean the end of fighting along the rivers. Small groups of Confederates, often with mobile artillery, appeared along the banks of the Mississippi and its tributaries and shot up any vessel not under convoy of one of the tinclads. The occurrence at Waterproof is described:

The dastardly character of the war on the part of the South has evinced itself in a thousand ways. Torpedoes in the rivers, on the roads, in works they lacked the means or courage to hold, have been used on one side only, and history will record, with stern condemnation, on which side.

Barbarism shows itself, too, in the constant attack on passenger boats and unarmed conveyances. The sketch portrayed by our Artist gives recent instance of this spirit. The guerillas have become very troublesome on the Mississippi. The Welcome, Captain Bryan, from St. Louis to New Orleans, with a cargo of Western products and cattle, as well as a number of passengers, including several ladies, among others Mrs. Crocker, wife of the General in command at Natchez, was attacked by guerillas about eight o'clock on Sunday, Nov. 22, while passing a place called Waterproof, below Vicksburg. Without warning, and regardless of the lives of

Ivonne stanching the wounds of the naval hero

The guerrilla war on the Mississippi. Explosion of a shell in the ladies' salon of the steamer *Welcome*, at Waterproof, Mississippi

women and children, these wretches poured volley after volley into her. In the short time that she was exposed, she received 11 cannon balls and 160 Minie bullets. One shell burst in the social hall, or ladies' cabin, tearing away the flooring and two doors and scattering the passengers in dismay. The wheel was struck and the pilot so alarmed that, but for the presence of Gen. Benton, who stood by, and regardless of a severe wound he received, directed his movements, the steamer would have been taken.

The men who conducted this type of operation were always called "guerillas" by the Northern press, and some of them would probably merit the term; but the majority belonged to perfectly regular commands, usually the cavalry of Forrest or Wheeler. Their procedure on these raids was to fan out, attacking anything weak enough to give a promise of easy booty or likely to damage Union communications. They were so much of a nuisance that by the end of 1863, 48 of the tinclads were constantly employed on convoy duty on the rivers, and probably as many as 75,000 men were scattered about in various posts to hold the main communications centers. The battles at Chattanooga sensibly reduced the menace by depriving the raiders of the fulcrum of an army.

No close reader of the contemporary weeklies can fail to be struck with the fact that a change came over them in the late fall of 1863 and the ensuing winter. Down to this date the war had been the major and almost the only interest, at least in the picture sections. But that fall the artists began to draw all sorts of scenes from civilian life, as though people had learned to live with the war and no longer regarded it as the central fact of life. As with the pictures, so with the copy; more space went to literary matters, a bridge accident in Chicago, honesty in

politics, a sale of color prints, and there were fewer biographies of prominent soldiers or reminiscent accounts of battles.

The huge ironclad ram *Dunderberg* was the only attempt on the part of the Union to construct a ship on the standard Confederate system, with a ram bow, low ends, and a sloping armored casements amidships. She really was something like the most powerful warship of her day, displacing 7000 tons and being armed with two 15-inch and eight 11-inch guns. The Confederate mistake of too-weak engines was avoided; she was given power intended to provide a speed of 15 knots, and almost made it.

In other respects also *Dunderberg* was pretty well ahead of her time. So far as there is a record, she was the first warship to be fitted with a double bottom, and the first to have a complete system of watertight bulkheads, both transverse and longitudinal. The armor on the hull was four and a half inches — considerable for those days.

She was laid down in July, 1862, but the builders immediately found themselves in the presence of a whole series of new problems and had to play by ear. As a result the huge ironclad was not completed until the middle of 1865, at which date the government found itself with the largest navy in the world and no particular use for it. The current theory was that of a navy for coast defense only, so *Dunderberg* became a disposable item and was sold to France. There she was named *Rochambeau*, and many of her features were copied in French ships.

There was probably no more futile campaign in the Civil War than that of Mine Run, when Meade crossed the Rapidan, started an attack, found the Confederates dug in, and after avoiding Lee's counterstroke simply went home again. This is the contemporary account:

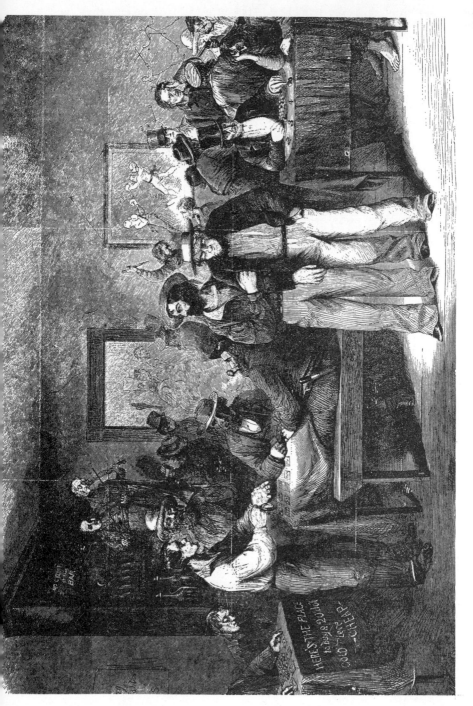

A gambling scene at Pike's Peak

The *Dunderberg*, the greatest man-of-war in the world, as she now appears in William H. Webb's shipyard

The Army of the Potomac at Mine Run. General Warren's troops attacking

On Monday evening the two armies were separated by Mine Run valley which crosses the Fredericksburg and Orange plank-road twelve miles from Orange Court House. General Lee is strongly intrenched there, and seems disposed to make a firm resistance. The dispatches of correspondents indicate that an assault on the enemy's works at Mine Run by our infantry, under cover of artillery, took place on Monday. All our batteries which could command the enemy's position were ordered to open, and after half an hour's firing, which the enemy feebly answered, an attack was ordered. General Warren pushed on, and found the number and position of the enemy stronger than anticipated, and paused for further instructions. The attack was then immediately checked, and all firing ceased. This is the latest story we have from the Army of the Potomac. Rebel accounts to Sunday say that the two armies were then confronting each other.

The pictorial reporting, as it often does, reflects the character of the campaign. Not reproduced are pictures of the countryside, of lines of trenches, of the ford by which the crossing was made—all essentially static, all carrying the message that nothing much had happened at Mine Run or could be expected to happen.

From Morris Island, General Gilmore, who occupied much more space in contemporary accounts than in subsequent history, continued to shell Fort Sumter and Charleston.

The latest news from Charleston states that General Gilmore was then shelling the city, throwing twenty shells a day, with considerable damage. All the inhabitants had ben removed to the rear of the city, the fire proving, it is presumed, destructive. The firing on Fort Sumter had been discontinued, but Fort Johnson and the other defenses inside the harbor were receiving a terrific fire from our batteries. The rebel flag which has heretofore floated over Fort Sumter is no longer displayed, and only an occasional shot is fired from the ruins. The rebels, it appears, have been erecting new batteries near Fort Moultrie, under cover of a hospital flag, which was respected by our forces, in accordance with the laws of war.

It is worth noting that the earlier complaisance about allowing artist-correspondents through the lines has by this time disappeared. Pictures from within the Confederacy bear the attribution: "By an English Artist."

*Above:* Interior of Fort Sumter after bombardment from Morris Island. *Below:*
Bursting of a shell in the streets of Charleston, South Carolina

Halt of a

wagon train

Sufferings in a snowstorm on the Michigan Central

One of the civilian events that attracted attention that winter was a little trouble with snow on the Michigan Central:

The Michigan Central, due at Chicago at half past 10 o'clock in the evening, proceeded with considerable difficulty for seven miles—a distance which it was able to reach only at 6 o'clock the next morning—when the train plunged into an immense drift which barred all further progress. The situation was one of great peril, and the only hope of rescue lay in the arrival of the Michigan Southern train, which must cross the track of the Central Road at a distance of four hundred yards from where the train was embedded. Over a hundred passengers occupied the three passenger cars, and many of them were women and children, besides two wounded soldiers. The fires were almost out, and if not replenished there was no escape from a frozen death.

Strong men nerved themselves for the emergency, and, digging through snow-banks ten feet in depth, found some fence rails, which they brought on board for fuel. But out of this momentary relief arose a fresh disaster. The violent draft of wind through the burning pine soon brought the stoves and pipes to a red heat, and the roof of one of the cars was shortly in a blaze. If the flames were not put out, every car was doomed, as it was impossible to separate one from another. Both men and women fought the flames with snow, until at length they were thoroughly subdued. Then again, after the menace of the fire, came that of the bitter cold. The roof had been burned off, and wind and snow beat in without mercy. This car was no longer tenable, and into the other two the hundred passengers had hardly been crowded when one of these was on fire. Again the enemy was fought and baffled; but again it was necessary for the entire company to transfer themselves to the single remaining car. It was now 2 o'clock in the afternoon. No help was at hand and after the exhausting labors of the forenoon the passengers seemed resigned to indifference, as if their fate was settled. But the hoped-for train came at last, and stopped for the sufferers of this miserable land-wreck.

The question of prisoners of war became increasingly tense that winter. Grant had paroled most of those he took at Vicksburg, but the Southern conscription laws did not allow them to keep their paroles, and he captured some of the same men at Chattanooga. In addition, the Confederacy absolutely refused to exchange Negro soldiers or white officers in command of them; and when the Union authorities refused any exchange unless Negroes were included, the Confederates declined to receive rations for Union prisoners, who were, in truth, on a starvation diet. Throughout the winter the press gave a good deal of attention to the prisoner question, but it was never satisfactorily settled.

*Be it resolved* by the Senate and House of Representatives of the United States of America in Congress assembled, That the thanks of Congress be and they hereby are presented to Major-General Ulysses S. Grant, and through him to the officers and soldiers who have fought under his command during the rebellion, for their gallantry and good conduct in the battles in which they have engaged; and that the President of the United States be requested to cause a Gold Medal to be struck, with suitable emblems, devices and inscriptions, to be presented to Major-General Grant.

Section 2. *And be it further resolved,* That, when said Medal shall have been struck, the President shall cause a copy of this joint resolution to be engrossed on parchment, and shall transmit the same, together with the said Medal, to Major-General Grant, to be presented

The war in Tennessee. Bivouac of Rebel prisoners on an island near Bridgeport, Tennessee

Thanks to Grant

to him in the name of the people of the United States of America.

Section 3. *And be it further resolved,* That a sufficient sum of money to carry this resolution into effect is hereby appropriated out of any money in the Treasury not otherwise appropriated.

*(Passed unanimously and without opposition in both Houses: Approved by the President and the Country.)*

No other comment was offered at the time; and none other was necessary.

The naval war occupied a good deal of attention from the weeklies, perhaps even a disproportionate amount of attention, mainly because ships make such good pictures. The drawing was generally accurate; it was fairly easy to sketch a ship at rest and place her in the required position of action.

Blockade-running remained big business right down to the end of the war. It was aided by a little-remembered fact: there were no searchlights. The blockade-runner thus had to be right on top of one of the cordon of blockaders on a dark night before she was sighted. Mostly it was a business of stealth rather than speed. Blockade-runners were usually British-built and were made as fast as possible; but as early as 1862 there began to appear in the blockading fleets the sloops and gunboats with engines designed by B. F. Isherwood. He was one of the greatest engineers of his or any other period, and a ship chased by one of his cruisers was usually caught.

The monitor *Weehawken* foundered off Charleston on December 6, 1863, as the result of a peculiar accident. The ventilation in this class of ships was as good as John Ericsson could make it, but even this was not very good, and *Weehawken* had her fore-hatch open as she lay at anchor during a mild gale accompanied by heavy swells. She shipped a heavy sea forward, which filled the cable and anchor wells. The ship was rolling so heavily that the crew amidships did not notice she was down by the head, more water got in, and before the bulkhead doors could be closed the ship was already moribund.

This class of monitors, the class immediately following the original one, were armed with one 15-inch gun,

The United States steamer *Kennebec* chasing the Rebel steamer *Grey Jacket*

The siege of Charleston. Sinking of the monitor *Weehawken*, December 7

firing solid shot, and an 11-inch rifle, firing shell. The latter was considered better for attacks on wooden ships and fortifications, the larger gun for firing at armor. A large number of monitors were built and several others begun but never finished; and none were ever quite as successful as the ten ships of the *Passaic* class, which immediately followed the original *Monitor* and were only a slight improvement on her design.

Interior of the turret of the monitor *Montauk*

*Leslie's*, which carried the picture of the auction of the gold piece, commented that it was bid for more for its cash value than as a numismatic item. It brought $150.

The shooting of Burroughs, whoever he was, is unrecorded by history. Contemporary account:

A few days ago a negro sentinel belonging to Colonel John A. Nelson's regiment shot Burroughs for attempting to escape from the small-pox hospital at Portsmouth, Virginia. We give a sketch representing this interesting incident. Burroughs was captured shortly after Butler assumed command of the Department, was tried, and sentenced to death as a guerila; and while awaiting execution was seized with the small-pox and conveyed to the hospital. Colonel Wheldon, upon his convalescence, gave orders for his removal to the jail; but the Lieutenant commissioned to execute those orders brought no warrant, and was refused admission by the sentinel, who was a negro. Burroughs, supposing from the altercation that friends had come to his assistance, tried to escape through the window. On hearing the noise the sentinel opened the door, and seeing the prisoner in the act of passing out, fired and killed him.

One of the great American sports is selecting Presidential candidates before the time comes to choose them officially. *Harper's* got into this game in its first issue of 1864 and this is what it said:

The gentlemen whose accession to political power depends upon the salvation of slavery are already casting about for available Presidential candidates. A year ago the nomination of Mr. Horatio Seymour was a foregone conclusion. But his obsequiousness to a murderous mob alarmed

The money crisis in the South. Auction sale of a five-dollar gold piece at Danville, near the North Carolina border

The Negro sentinel shooting the guerrilla Burroughs

Headquarters of the United States Sanitary Commission at Gettysburg,
Pennsylvania

the most substantial of his supporters. They hate Abolitionism; but a civil magistrate who calls the most reckless and brutal criminals his friends appalls them. Mr. Seymour, so long as he made dull speeches merely, was to have been nominated as "a Conservative statesman." But Conservative statesmanship in practical operation during the days of July was a little too repugnant to the popular common-sense. The Conservative statesman committed political suicide upon the steps of the City Hall. His alternate, if circumstances should require a military candidate, was General M'Clellan.

Poor General M'Clellan! He held his tongue while every friend of the rebels praised him and every loyal man looked on in painful doubt. But when the Pennsylvania election came, and the rebel papers prayed for the success of Woodward, and Lee moved to support his chances, and the lackeys of slavery and rebel partisans strained every nerve for Woodward, and every loyal Union man in the land knew that his election would be equivalent to a victory over the Army of the Potomac, then the late leader of that army chose to break his long silence by declaring that Woodward was the candidate for him. Poor General M'Clellan! His letter was as fatal to his political hopes as Governor Seymour's speech.

The moment General M'Clellan subordinated his military conduct to his political aspirations he was doomed. A more tragical campaign than his upon the Peninsula history does not record. Not three volumes of a thousand pages each can explain away the prolonged horrors of the Chickahominy swamps. It was the penalty of not comprehending the war. He thought he could fight without hurting the enemy much; for it would not do to exasperate one's natural political allies. He would try fighting with one hand and waving the olive branch with the other.

Does any body suppose that the same game can be played with General Grant? General Grant is a soldier who does not believe in olive branches but in unconditional surrender. His politics are the overthrow of the rebel army in the field, and the destruction of the cause that sends it there. The revolutionary Tories in Connecticut would as soon have nomi-

The assassin foiled

nated Israel Putnam for Governor as the Copperheads of to-day would wish General Grant for President. And from whom then is his support to come?

Certainly not from the friends of the Government; for hearty and unconditional as is their admiration for General Grant's military services, they have no less regard for the civil services of Mr. Lincoln. No man at this moment has so sure a hold of the national heart as the President. It would as soon think of removing General Grant from command of his great army, because he is conquering the rebel host, as it would of setting aside Mr. Lincoln because his administration is restoring the Union. If the Presidential election took place next week, Mr. Lincoln would undoubtedly be returned by a greater majority than any President since Washington. And unless he is deserted by his great sagacity, or some huge military disaster befalls the country, or some serious blunder is committed by the Union men in Congress, his election is as sure as the triumph of the nation over the rebellion.

3RD CORPS BADGE

GOING TO THE BALL

BALL ROOM.

THE SUPPER ROOM

THE GANDERS.

This is pretty good experting, although things were to grow a little more dubious later in the year, when Grant was stopped at Petersburg and Sherman appeared to be stopped before Atlanta. But the most interesting thing about it is the reversal on McClellan. Turn back the pages; see what the same weekly had to say about the same general on the occasion of his dismissal from the command of the Army of the Potomac. The point is that at the earlier date he was still regarded as a purely military personality; by the later one he had injected himself into the political situation, and his military acts came under review in the light of his expressed ambitions.

One tends to think of war, or has been instructed to think of it in terms of mud, filth, wounds, and boredom, only occasionally elevated by high heroic ardors. To the soldiers of the Army of the Potomac it was not so; they often had fun. The higher command rather frowned on gambling as a means of amusement and it was not unusual for gamblers to be drummed out of camp, but dances were different. The III Corps gave a big one, thus described:

Our Army of the Potomac, taking advantage of the cessation of hostilities during the winter, indulges now and then in a festive entertainment. The presence of soldiers' wives with their husbands in camp gives, of course, the crowning charm to these gatherings. We present our readers with a sketch of a ball lately given by the Third Army Corps. While the fortunate soldiers who have partners are at supper with their ladies, those not so successful are engaged in what is called the "gander" dance.

Paris fashions, winter 1863-64

The stag dance

The ball was quite a success; a score of Generals attended; and it was altogether an event to break up the monotony of every-day dreariness in camp. It was the first opportunity that gave the ladies staying in camp with their husbands a chance to come together.

Later there was another kind of dance, described:

Our soldiers believe in the literal interpretaion of the dictum of the Wise Man that "there is a time to dance." But to put their faith into works is not the easiest thing in the world, owing to the lack of partners of the feminine persuasion. However, by imagining a bearded and pantallooned fellow to be of "t'other kind," they succeed in getting up what they call a "Stag Dance," which is better than none.

A curious feature of almost any given war is how it brings into prominence for strictly strategic reasons certain places which have no particular previous or subsequent history. Matamoros was one of these; it was the depot through which French and British supplies (exceedingly well paid for, it may be noted) poured into the Confederacy, and after the fall of Vicksburg, into the Trans-Mississippi area.

Governor Seymour of New York opposed the draft with an energy that was a reflection of the great riots and the state of mind among voters. Nevertheless the quotas had to be met, and unless they were met by volunteering, the men would have to be drafted. The state thus became one of those that appropriated considerable sums for bounties, and it was heartily backed by the city.

Out of this grew a new profession —that of "bounty-jumping." It was much less easy to exercise than one might think; the rear areas of the Army of the Potomac were full of patrols and check points which soldiers going in the wrong direction had to pass, and the bridges at Washington were well guarded. Still the professionals did work at it, usually try-

Scenes on the Rio Grande

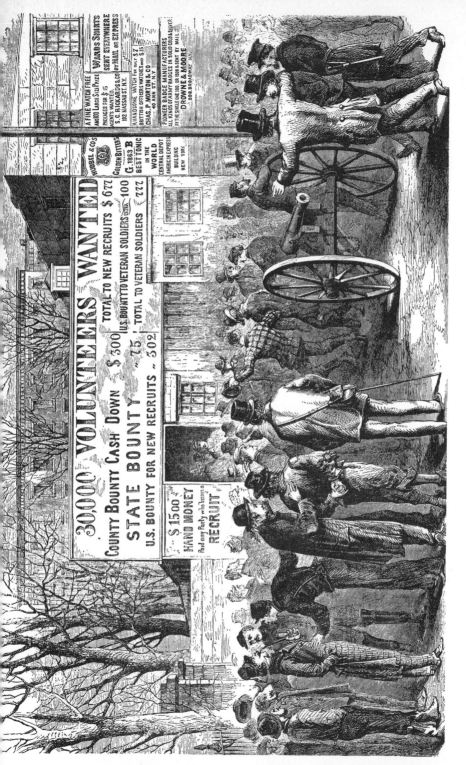

Recruiting for the war. Scene at the recruiting tents in the park, New York

Snowy morning. On picket

ing to get free at some point between the recruiting office and the front line, and they even developed a loose organization which knew the best methods and the right people to bribe.

This brought on the scene an individual whose very existence was unknown to the contemporary press: the formidable and unscrupulous Lafayette Baker, War Department detective and counterespionage agent. The stories that grew up around him are legion; he told the best ones himself and at least part of them are true. By 1864 he had so hampered the Confederate espionage service in Washington that it functioned only irregularly and inefficiently; and early in that year he scored a stunning coup over the bounty-jumper organization.

Baker was proud of his prowess at disguise; he succeeded in working his way into the ring, and once in explained how easy it would be to organize the whole thing more efficiently. The result was a kind of bounty-jumpers' convention, attended not only by the bounty-jumpers themselves, but by Baker and his agents. Over 70 of them went to jail, and it was characteristic of Baker that this

did not make the papers either, because he had them tried secretly by military commissions and clapped into forts.

The park in the recruiting picture is not Central Park, but the one surrounding City Hall. Recruiting was originally done in tents; the building erected for the purpose was still called "the tents."

The hospital train was a new invention:

Until very recently the transportation of our sick and wounded soldiers by rail has been attended with very severe suffering from the jostling motion of the car. It first occurred to a surgeon, while witnessing the intense agony of these poor fellows, that the difficulty might be obviated by mechanical means. Directly and on the spot he sketched the model of a car, in the contrivance of which the problem was satisfactorily solved. The plan was adopted by the Government, and now constitutes the prominent feature of the hospital train. The wounded men are taken directly to the hospital upon the same stretchers which answer as couches upon the car. These beds are suspended from India-rubber bands attached to the framework of the car, and, yielding to the slightest motion of the car, are as comfortable as the beds of the hospital.

The interior of a hospital car

Libby Prison in Richmond was mostly used for officers. In December, 1863, a considerable group of them started work on that favorite occupation of war prisoners: an escape by tunneling. In groups of 12 they were lowered through the chimney into the cellar, where they began to dig, using fingers, knives, chisels, or anything else that came to hand.

For fifty-one days they worked away at the tunnel—the dirt being hid under the refuse and straw on the floor. When it was impossible any longer to throw the dirt out by hand a spitoon was used as a dirt-cart, being attached to a string on either side and drawn to and from the cellar. After patiently working in this manner for a number of days they came to a point

under an out-house across the way, which was used as a depository for parcels sent from the North, and began to dig upward. The prisoners started out on the evening of February 9th, in small squads, each taking different routes. At two o'clock the lights of the city were put out and escape was more feasible. In their efforts to reach the Union lines some were recaptured; but out of the one hundred and nine who attempted this adventure, the greater number suceeded. They were aided by negroes, by Union citizens, and by cavalry detachments sent out by General Butler for that purpose as soon as he heard of the escape.

The Libby Prison delivery made an immense noise in the press at the time—fallen very silent now; but at the time it was one of the few noted events while artillery was struggling through the mud and everyone was waiting the opening of the spring campaigns. One other event of the period received a big press: the raid toward Richmond of a wing of Kilpatrick's cavalry, 400 of whom were under Colonel Ulric Dahlgren, son of the admiral.

The contemporary account tells the story:

"A prisoner states that a Colonel with one foot has been captured," said the first report of Kilpatrick's raid.

"A rebel deserter informs one of my Aids that a one-legged Colonel and about a hundred men were taken prisoners," telegraphed General Butler to the President.

The escaped refugees from the Libby Prison

Escaping Union officers succored by slaves

"Of one thing the public may rest assured that these officers will escape if such a thing is within the region of possibilities," said a later account.

"Colonel Dahlgren is dead," said yet another report.

Ulric Dahlgren is scarcely more than twenty years old. He was wounded in the leg last summer, just after the battle of Gettysburg, in the daring dash by which he succeeded in capturing the rebel dispatches from Jefferson Davis to General Lee. His leg was subsequently taken off. Four weeks ago he was a tall, slight, pale-faced boy, sitting quietly in Washington and saying pleasantly, "I am waiting for my new leg, and then I shall see whether I can ride again." Four weeks ago! We all know now whether he can ride again. The brave boy has not only dashed at the outworks of the rebel city, but, living or dead, he has ridden straight into the love and honor of his countrymen.

He was dead, and the death was something of a personal tragedy to Lincoln, who had known him well. But the tragedy only serves to outline a fact too little noticed about the Civil War, and it was a key fact. That fact is the growing tendency toward youth in the upper officer ranks of the Union Army. There were young men in the Confederate Army, too, but it is nevertheless true that the upper officers—Lee, Johnston, Hood, the two Hills, Ewell, Hardee, Stuart—were men who had started the war at the top, and largely older men.

In the Union Army the older men had failed and disappeared. Not that Grant, Sherman, Warren, Thomas, Sedgwick, and Hancock were precisely youngsters; but their age average was perceptibly below that of their Confederate opposite numbers. And beneath them there were beginning to emerge the group of really young officers—Sheridan, in his early 30's; Custer, Upton, Merritt, in their 20's and already general officers; Wilson, who at the age of 27 was to command an independent army, younger

Ambuscade and death of Colonel Dahlgren

Dragging artillery through the mud

Soldiers' ball at Huntsville, Alabama. Dancing the Virginia Reel

Major General William T. Sherman

than any man in history except Napoleon and Alexander the Great.

How much influence this had on the war might be a subject of some study. At the time there was no sign that anybody thought about the matter. The Union only knew that it was getting some very young officers, including colonels not yet old enough to vote.

Early in 1864 the illustrated press began to print pictures of an extremely hard-faced officer with a bristling beard: William Tecumseh Sherman. At least one foreign observer had already set it down that he would be the most dangerous opponent the South had, but as yet the North knew little about him.

*Harper's* gave a few bald biographical details and went on:

Appointed a Brigadier-General he succeeded General Anderson in command of the Department of the Ohio. He was removed because he said that 200,000 men would be needed to fight the rebels successfully in Kentucky. This statement—afterward found to be true—was at that time suggestive of insanity.

When Congress passed the bill reviving the rank of lieutenant-general everyone knew who it was for, and the event was reported without emotion or any particular comment. Grant's own completely unassuming demeanor did not give the correspondents much to work on either. There had to be a picture of him receiving his commission, of course, but the reporting was cold:

It is intimated, in well-informed quarters, that important movements will soon be made. General Grant visited Washington on the 8th instant, and had a conference with the Secretary of War and General Halleck, and subsequently had an important consultation with General Meade at the head-quarters of the Army of the Potomac, whence he returned on the 11th, and immediately started for the West. He will, it is probable, direct a movement of all our armies according to a plan of his own. Preparatory to any movement in the East, it is hinted that the Army of the Potomac will be reorganized. On the 14th inst. the President issued an order retiring Major-General Halleck from the position of General-in-Chief, and assigning Lieutenant-General Grant to the command of the armies of the United States, with head-quarters in Washington, and also with the Lieutenant-General in

General Grant receiving his commission as Lieutenant General from President Lincoln

Negroes leaving their home

the field. General Halleck is to be chief of staff under the Secretary of War and the Lieutenant-General. Major-General W. T. Sherman is to command the military division of the Mississippi, comprising the Departments of the Ohio, the Cumberland, the Tennessee, and the Arkansas. Major-General McPherson is placed in command of the Department and army of the Tennessee.

That was all. The weekly was a great deal interested that week in a letter in which Chase asked that his name be not used as a candidate for the presidency; in a manifesto by the Tammany "War Democracy"; in the fact that John C. Frémont was injecting himself into the Presidential campaign. It was somewhat more mildly interested in the overcrowding of New York buses and streetcars, and it commented feelingly on the fact that the 1st Division of the II Corps had formed a Lecture Association and invited speakers. For Grant it did not have much time.

The view [above] illustrates a phase of the war which the rebels have found it difficult to contemplate with any complacency. The exodus of the slaves from the bondage which has so long oppressed them has been steady and continuous from the moment the first blow was struck against the national honor, and it still goes on, hundreds and thousands of the poor, outraged creatures coming weekly into the Union lines at all points in the field. Our sketch gives an admirable view of the desolation which surrounds the homes of the negroes, and the heartiness and energy with which they make their way to freedom upon the slightest opportunity. The Federal gun-boat, it will be seen, lies far out at sea, but the sharp eyes of the waiting, watching bond-men have caught sight of the flag she carries; they know there is shelter under it for them, and launching their little boat, they carefully put the aged and infirm, with their few more valuable effects, aboard, and with a pang, it may be, at leaving their rude home, but with hope and joy in their hearts at the prospects of deliverance, pull away from the shore, which henceforth, is to be to them only a dark, dreary line marking a yet darker past.

In 1864 the spring campaign was everywhere late in getting under way,

Ladies in attendance in regulation costume at the Metropolitan Fair

Admiral Porter's flotilla

and the great Metropolitan Fair stole the show from the soldiers. It was held for the benefit of the Sanitary Commission in several buildings on Union Square and 14th Street and seems to have attracted visitors from a considerable area. There was an Indian wigwam, where one could "study the habits and peculiarities of the aborigines," who put on a war dance "to the intense gratification of the spectators." There was a good-sized book department, and a boat-building department, with small craft in various stages of construction and the walls copiously lined with models.

But the big play went to the Department of Arms and Trophies. "Much interest is manifested in the two handsome swords—one of which is to be presented to a navy and the other to an army officer. The swords cost $1500 each"; the public was invited to subscribe, each dollar turned in entitling the giver to one vote as to who should get the swords. (There is no record of who did.) The total number of other arms and trophies was carefully set down at 1022, and included not only current items such

as the battle flags of New York regiments but also "tomahawks, rapiers, Sandwich Island daggers and Indian arrows," in addition to the authentic sword surrendered to Gates by Burgoyne at Saratoga, a spur worn by Major André, and the first bowie knife ever made. No doubt was expressed as to the genuineness of any of the relics.

Grant's original plan of campaign was a series of simultaneous movements—by the Army of the Potomac against Lee, by Butler's Army of the James direct on Richmond, by the Army of the Shenandoah up the valley, by Sherman toward Atlanta and by Banks from New Orleans against Mobile. This was whittled down by politics, and instead of moving on Mobile, Banks started early and up the Red River toward Shreveport, Louisiana, with the support of Admiral Porter's gunboats.

Fort De Russy was reached on March 15 and taken without a fight, whereupon the real animus of the

The opening of the Red River region has placed within our reach a vast amount of cotton, which the enemy had stored

Repulse of the Rebels at Pleasant Hill, Louisiana

Rebel attack on our gunboats in the Red River

away for export or sale. On the 17th 800 bales from near Fort De Russy reached Cairo, and large quantities were still awaiting transportation at the date of our last advices. In the vicinity of Shreveport thousands of bales are believed to be hidden away; and should our army arrive in time to prevent its destruction a large sum must be realized from this source. While thus weakening the rebels in the seizure of one of their main elements of strength, the advance of the Federal forces has also achieved a vast positive advantage in delivering the loyal people from the oppression which has so long restrained them.

That is, it was at least partly a cotton hunt, and immensely profitable to anyone who could get a finger in the pie. The contemporary running account mentions, without emphasizing this, and continues:

The armies of Generals A. J. Smith and Banks have effected a junction at Alexandria, Louisiana, the enemy retreating to Shreveport by land. Our gun-boats seized over 4000 bales of cotton, and vast quantities were still coming in. Two steamers, with 3000 bales of cotton, were burned by the rebels to prevent their falling into our hands.

The next report was of a "battle" in which 18 were killed, and all was going well. Then comes:

The Red River expedition has met with disaster. Advancing from Alexandria toward Shreveport, General Banks' army passed through Grand Ecore, sixty miles from Alexandria, on April 6, the fleet having, meanwhile, got within one hundred miles of Shreveport. On the 8th our cavalry, after driving the enemy for two days, were attacked in force at Pleasant Hill, De Soto Parish, Louisiana, and infantry coming up, a stubborn battle ensued, resulting in the rout of our whole force. The Nineteenth Army Corps finally came up and checked the enemy, who were 10,000 strong. Our loss was over 2000. The enemy also lost heavily. The army fell back to Grand Ecore, and would there reorganize. At last accounts Alexandria was strongly defended.

This is an extremely curious account, chiefly remarkable for its lacunae. There was no attempt to cover the fact of defeat, but just about everything else was as wrong as it could be. The battle was not at Pleasant Hill but at Sabine Cross Roads, and the extremely unusual error of underestimating the enemy's force has been made. (Both these were corrected the following week.) Also, there is not even a hint of what really happened at Sabine Cross Roads, which was that Banks conducted his march so incompetently that the Confederates roughed up his flank and captured his wagon train.

He began to retreat at once, and in the real Battle of Pleasant Hill, several days later, the one pictured here, the Confederates were effectively stopped, mostly by some of Sherman's veterans under A. J. "Whiskey" Smith. The artist-correspondent caught it, but there was not a word from the writing men. The next report:

News from the Red River to the 19th of April is to the effect that General Banks, having strongly fortified Grand Ecore, had marched out to meet the rebels, and that skirmishing had been in progress for some days. Reinforcements for General Banks' army were going forward.

This was straight out of the domain of fantasy. Banks had not fortified Grand Ecore; he had not marched out to meet the rebels, but was retreating as fast as he could, over the protests of his subordinate generals, one of whom tried to get the rest to join him in relieving Banks and placing him under arrest. Nathaniel P. Banks, that politically important officer, was in a state of complete funk, and he must have realized as clearly as anybody that both campaign and reputation were ruined.

But the center of gravity was no longer in either Banks or his retreating army. It was in the 19 gunboats and monitors, the best in the Mississippi squadron, brought up the river by Admiral Porter. Something peculiar happened that spring. Although the Mississippi was exceptionally high, the Red River did not rise at all, for the first time since 1855. The result was that the water was so low that the question of saving the ships became urgent, especially getting them through the rapids known as the Falls of Alexandria. Porter wanted Banks to

Porter's gunboats passing the dam in the Red River, near Alexandria

make a stand at that place, but Banks answered only in double-talk and it was evident that he had no other intentions than further retreat.

"At the last accounts our position at Alexandria was secure, and the gunboats in the Red River above the Falls, where they were detained by the low water, were still safe, though greatly harassed by the enemy."

This was taking place above Alexandria, where the Confederates came down to the banks with infantry and artillery to shoot up the little tinclads covering the rear. There was a memorable battle against the little *Cricket*, smallest of the tinclads, with Porter himself aboard. She was suddenly attacked from ambush by at least 18 heavy guns and in a few minutes lost 31 men out of a crew of 50, including all her firemen and most of the gunners. Porter himself went to the pilothouse and conned the drifting vessel downstream, where she escaped thanks to the work of emergency gun crews and the lucky accident of meeting another gunboat coming up to see what the shooting was about.

The artist evidently drew his picture of the occasion from description; he has shown the slope-sided ironclads which were the most prominent ships on the rivers instead of the tinclads, quite different vessels.

But this escape was only an escape; the problem remained of getting the big ships past the rapids, with Banks as doughty as ever in his determination to retreat, although he had not been attacked. At this point there appeared one Colonel Joseph Bailey of the 4th Wisconsin, who had been a lumberman and remembered that logs were floated downstream on artificial freshets created by damming.

Banks agreed to detail men to build a dam and Bailey took charge. They were woodsmen, but not, as is usually supposed and sometimes stated from the Northwest; they were three regiments from Northern New York and one from Maine. In a surprisingly short time they cut down a forest of trees and took mills apart for beams, while all the forges in the fleet made heavy iron bolts for ties, and the armor was taken off most of the ironclads. The center of the dam broke through before it was completed, but the ships rode down to safety. The event was reported clearly but without much comprehension:

A dispatch from Admiral Porter states that the portion of his squadron above the falls at Alexandria have been released from their unpleasant position, owing to the indefatigable exertions of Colonel Bailey, who proposed and built a tree-dam of 600 feet across the river at the lower falls, which enabled the vessels to pass in safety, the back water of the Mississippi reaching Alexandria, and allowing them to pass over all the shoals and the obstructions planted by the enemy to a point of safety.

It is a pity that the style of our tradition has caused this story of a rescue so nearly to drop from our history. Americans like unalloyed success.

A fact that needs recognition as historical, even though unpleasant, is that the South never gave up on its bitterness on the Northern employment of Negroes as soldiers. The matter came to a head at Fort Pillow, reported thus:

On the 12th inst. the rebel General Forrest appeared before Fort Pillow, near Columbus, Kentucky, attacking it with considerable vehemence. This was followed up by frequent demands for its surrender, which were refused by Major Booth, who commanded the fort. The fight was then continued up until 3 P.M., when Major Booth was killed, and the rebels, in large numbers, swarmed over the intrenchments. Up to that time comparatively few of our men had been killed; but immediately upon occupying the place

Negroes escaping out of slavery

Foraging in Louisiana

The massacre at Fort Pillow

the rebels commenced an indiscriminate butchery of the whites and blacks, including the wounded. Both white and black were bayonetted, shot or sabred; even dead bodies were horribly mutilated, and children of seven and eight years, and several negro women killed in cold blood. Soldiers unable to speak from wounds were shot dead, and their bodies rolled down the banks into the river. The dead and wounded negroes were piled in heaps and burned, and several citizens, who had joined our forces for protection, were killed or wounded. Out of the garrison of six hundred only two hundred remained alive. Three hundred of those massacred were negroes; five were buried alive. Six guns were captured by the rebels, and carried off, including two 10-pound Parrotts, and two 12-pound howitzers.

To this account history has had little to add, and in fact Forrest sent in an official report that was practically an admission. It said:

"The approximate loss was 500 killed, but few of the officers escaped. It is hoped that these facts will demonstrate to the northern people that the negro soldier cannot cope with Southerners."

The affair caused an immense sensation in the press, a special congressional investigating committee, and a meeting of the Cabinet, at which retaliation was discussed and written opinions given. Nothing was done. . . .

Most particularly in forward areas like Louisiana, the government rations were never adequate, and foraging from farms was freely resorted to. This resulted in a long series of claims which were in the courts for many years after the war and seldom settled to anyone's satisfaction.

The copy with the picture of the Union scout tells its own story:

We give a sketch illustrating an interesting phase of the war in Louisiana. Among the most useful auxiliaries of General Banks, in his operations in that State, is a band of native Scouts, led by Captain Dudley, who, knowing the country and accustomed to danger, penetrate every where in search of information. Many of these scouts are desperate men, who have suffered all manner of outrage at the hands of the enemy, and who, on this account, lose no opportunity to inflict the heaviest punishment on those who have driven them to the shelter of the swamps and forests. Captain Dudley is described as a slight, wiry man, about forty-five years old, with a small eye which is all black and a face which strikes one as full of cunning. A correspondent says of him: "He told me that he had been a physician on the Calcasien River; that he escaped the conscription, and had been living a wandering life for three years; that he had been back and forth from the Rio Grande to Mobile, had always escaped wounds, and I think had not even been shot at. One of his men told me that one night he followed a party of conscript-hunters to their camp, waited till they were asleep, then crawled among them, determined to capture a gun he had taken a liking to. One of the party waked, and Dudley lay down quietly among them until his hunter fell asleep, then helped himself to the gun, and 'silently passed away.'"

There must have been many similar but unrecorded characters.

The stories of all the rebel rams had curious elements, but that of *Albemarle* was the strangest of all. She was built far up the Roanoke River in an open cornfield by J. W. Cooke of the Confederate Navy, who took up railroad tracks to make her armor. It was unusually thick for a Confederate ironclad, nearly 6 inches. The only guns he could get were two 100-pound rifles from Richmond, but he equipped her with these and came down the river to Plymouth, where the Union had had a post ever since the invasion of the Carolina sounds.

Commander C. W. Flusser had charge of the Union ships in that area, which consisted of two vessels: *Southfield,* a converted ferryboat, and *Miami,* one of the double-enders built on the ferryboat pattern. Both were of wood. Flusser had asked in vain for reinforcements and, knowing all about the Confederate ram, could only do his best to handle her. His best was to link his two ships together with booms and heavy chains; the idea was to catch *Albemarle* between them, swing in on her, then board and fire through her upper deck, while other

Union scouts in Louisiana

The Rebel ram attacking Federal gunboats at Plymouth, North Carolina

boarders threw powder down her funnel.

It was a rather desperate plan and doomed to failure by the fact that the Confederate espionage service in that area was quite as good as the Union. When the ram came downstream on April 19, 1864, Captain Cooke knew all about Flusser's plan. He kept so close to the bank that the Union vessels could not get *Albemarle* between them, and drove his ram into *Southfield's* side. She sank so fast that she carried the prow of *Albemarle* down until water came in the forward gun port, but the ram pulled free and got alongside *Miami*. Captain Flusser himself aimed the big rifle which was his main armament at her; the shell he fired rebounded and killed him, and the marines who tried the boarding experiment fell off the sloping sides of the ironclad and were crushed between the two. *Miami* pulled out; Cooke failed to hit her with his two guns and had not speed enough to chase.

Reinforcements were sent into the sounds, but the Union trouble was that there was nothing sheathed with iron that had a shallow enough draft to get in, so the squadron that met *Albemarle* on the renewal of the conflict on May 5 consisted of four wooden double-enders: *Mattabessett, Wyalusing, Sassacus,* and *Miami.* One carried a spar torpedo; all had nets to foul the ram's propellers. The fight lasted all afternoon, and the Union ships were badly battered, with many casualties. The ram had a bad leak and that chronic disease of Confederate rams, trouble with her engines, so she steamed back up the river for repairs. But there was to be a good deal more to this story.

The contemporary account of *Albemarle's* first battle is full, fair, and surprisingly objective; it relates the death of Flusser, just as it occurred, and the retreat of *Miami.* The account of the May 5 fight, too long to quote, is in almost startling contrast. It does not name the ships engaged, says nothing of how the battle went off, and ends: "Crestfallen and defeated, he sought refuge in the river from which he had so vauntingly sallied." Apparently two quite different reporters were at work. The picture coverage of the second fight was also substandard and quite evidently produced by artists who did not see the

Union ships until after the battle and never saw *Albemarle* at all.

Photographs have made most people familiar with the clutter in the rear areas of a modern army. In the Civil War it was much the same. It is true that this was not promoted by such devices as tanks and self-propelled guns needing repair. But there were countless wagons, probably more of them than a modern army has trucks, since their capacity was less and their movements slower. There were ambulances and the equipment of the sutlers who sold all sorts of things to soldiers. All these meant workshops, in addition to those for repairing weapons. Each corps usually had its own. The chief difference from the modern scene was that this rear-area activity almost never attracted the attention of the artists. The material was too static for them; they left it to the photographers.

On May 3, 1864, Grant took the Army of the Potomac across the Rapidan and the desperate battles that were to last nearly all summer began. Early in the game the news was well behind the event. It was the night of May 6 before a single reporter reached Washington aboard a locomotive and gave the first news of the Wilderness to Lincoln and Stanton in person.

Both the daily and the weekly press quickly caught up, however. The dispatches became very long, very detailed, and generally very accurate. There was no attempt to gloss over the heavy losses or the character of the fighting; indeed, they could hardly be glossed over, for Washington was so filling up with wounded as to resemble a hospital city. The picture coverage, when it began (it seems to have been very difficult for artist-correspondents to get their material out), was quite as ample as the verbal, and if not always quite as good, this was because several new artists had evidently just been taken on and were being broken in.

Grant's famous dispatch: "We have now ended the sixth day of very heavy fighting. Our losses have been heavy, as well as those of the enemy. I propose to fight it out on this line if it takes all summer"—received a big

Workshops. Headquarters, Army of the Potomac

Army of the Potomac. Sleeping

on their arms

Major General Wadsworth fighting in the wilderness

Army of the Potomac. Our wounded escaping from the fires in the wilderness

play and was accompanied by editorial treatment:

The history of the last fortnight is the story of a tremendous battle between the armies of the Union and of the rebellion. No man will complain that we are not making war in earnest. The rebels fight with valor and tanacity, and their own papers no longer deride the loyal army as the scum of creation, but confess that it fights with nerve and desperation. The face of General Grant is itself a victory. Its fixed resolution is terrible. At the West, and conspicuously at Vicksburg, when foiled in one way, he tried another. He did every thing but doubt or despond, and always carried his point at last.

At the end of May, last year, Grant made his brilliant march inland from the Mississippi. At once our papers announced the fall of Vicksburg. It was a premature exultation, and was followed by a corresponding doubt and depression. But on the 4th of July he finished his work, and Vicksburg fell. There has been the same eagerness now, and the same impatient hurrah. If the morning papers did not record a new victory there was a general inclination toward the same doubt. Yet every body knew that Grant had entered upon a campaign which would be long and must be bloody. Every body knew that Lee had expected the assault and had prepared himself for it, and would contest the ground inch by inch. At the end of ten days the advantage unquestionably remained with us. "But he has not taken Richmond!" whispered the desponding. No, for he aimed at Lee. Lee was Richmond. When Lee is driven, Richmond totters. When Lee is overcome, Richmond falls.

How grand the spectacle of the Potomac army, officers and men, inspired by one sublime purpose, and all worthy of each other! Every soldier trusts his commander, and every commander the General-in-Chief. There is a unity which that army has never known, a confidence which is unprecedented. It is based not merely on the prestige of success which surrounds the Lieutenant-General, but upon the result of his operations. If at the end of ten days Grant had not outfought Lee, certainly Lee had not outgeneraled Grant. The rebel was forced by arts as well as arms from two chosen positions.

This is a well-reasoned and reasonable editorial and shows that at least the editor of *Harper's* had an idea of two points not always appreciated at the time and even later. Grant's objective was not Richmond but Lee's army; and Grant was a much more skillful tactician than even some of his supporters have been willing to believe. The phrase "hammering campaign" has obscured the latter fact; but the process by which Grant steadily forced his opponent southward, taking the right-most corps out of line and swinging it around behind the rest, excites the admiration of military men. It is one of the most difficult operations of war, for the moving corps must pass through the reserve areas and across the supply lines of all the others while they are actively engaged. To keep Lee so busy that he could attempt no counterattack while the movements were in progress was precisely one of the reasons for the hammering.

The editor seems to have caught some sense of this, and also of the fact that Grant had brought a new kind of morale to the army. Its spirits had risen under Hooker, but then came Chancellorsville, and Meade's failure to pursue Lee after Gettysburg, his failure to attack all through the fall of 1863, had sent the thermometer down again. Now, after the first day of the Wilderness, the men knew they had a leader to lead them to battle, and one who could not be shaken by Lee's delicate manipulations. The editorial comment reflects the fact that at Spottsylvania the men shouted as Grant went by: "There's the man that won't take orders from Bobby Lee!" Very possibly the editor was aware of it; it was common practice for cor-

Army of the Potomac. General Warren rallying the Marylanders

Grant's great campaign. Stevens' battery at Cold Harbor

respondents to stay at the front for a while, then come in and give their observations verbally, and it was still more common for editors to get from relatives letters written by soldiers at the front.

The editorial, internal evidence shows, was written ten days after the campaign began. Neither weekly again commented upon Grant's campaign until July 18, when *Harper's* had this to say:

The masterly skill and tenacity of General Grant keeps the mind of the country firmly fixed upon the army and the war. The action of Congress and the resolution of the War Department in devising new means for recruiting the ranks and presenting an undiminished as well as undaunted front to the enemy, merely respond to the evident purpose of the country.

... after which it trails off into a discussion of recruiting and a denunciation of the Copperheads. The weeklies were letting the front-line dispatches speak for themselves, and devoting most of their editorial space to the coming Presidential election.

The dispatches from Sherman's front were not as full as those from the Army of the Potomac and received editorial comment:

Although so much nearer to Virginia than to Georgia that we have had daily more copious details of military movements from Meade than from Sherman, our friends of the Western army must not suppose that their course has not been followed with a sympathy and interest proportioned to the importance of their struggle. The crowds which have gathered at morning and evening around the bulletin-boards have beheld with the same joy and pride the big black letters which announced Sherman's successful progress; the withdrawal from Dalton; the evacuation of Resaca; the capture of prisoners, guns, and trains.

The first news was:

Sherman, simultaneously with Grant's advance Richmondward, moved on Dalton in three columns; Thomas in front,

Army of the Potomac. The struggle for the salient,

near Spottsylvania, Virginia, May 12, 1864

Schofield from Cleveland on the north-east, while M'Pherson threw himself on the line of communication southwest at Resaca, fifteen miles south of Dalton. On Saturday the 7th, Thomas occupied Tunnel Hill, ten miles northwest of Dalton, and took up a strong position at Buzzard's Roost. By the flank movement on Resaca, Johnston was forced to evacuate Dalton. On Sunday the 15th, a battle was fought at Resaca, in which Sherman states his losses to have been 3000. Sherman captured Resaca on Monday the 16th, with 10 guns and 1200 prisoners.

This is clear and pretty accurate reporting, even if not very "copious." The picture coverage was good, too; *Harper's* had Theodore Davis with Sherman, one of the few artists they thought enough of to accord a signature.

The editor must have jacked his correspondent up a little; the next account is a pretty full one of the Battle of Resaca. Then comes:

General Sherman's march is still onward. Our record last week closed with the occupation of Kingston and the line of the Etowah River by our forces on the 19th ult. From that point on the 24th, having brought up his supplies, General Sherman resumed his march, pushing in a southwesterly direction for Altoona. Flanking the position, which is said to be even stronger than Atlanta, the army pressed forward toward Dallas, lying some twenty miles almost directly south of Altoona. Here we came up with the en-

General Sherman's advance. Buzzard's Roost Pass, Georgia

Sherman's department. General Geary's assault on Dug Gap, Georgia

emy, and on Saturday the 28th, an engagement took place between them and M'Pherson's corps, in which the rebels were driven back, with a loss to them of 2500 killed and wounded left in our hands, and about 300 prisoners.

This was true, but the curious thing about if was that it missed all the essential points. There is no mention of the Adairsville maneuver, where Sherman so nearly trapped Johnston in a double envelopment while Johnston thought he was trapping Sherman. Allatoona is spelled wrong; there is no word about the heavy fighting at Johnston's trench lines around Dallas, and most especially there is nothing about the remarkable feat of Sherman's army in rebuilding the rail line behind its advance so rapidly that men on the firing line could hear the whistle of the approaching engines in the rear.

Also, even the correspondents marching across the map with the army were aware that Sherman was steadily pushing forward, but there seems to have been no appreciation

of the fact that they were witnessing something remarkable in the way of maneuver, of flanking operations. The military difficulty with such sweeps is that they afford so many opportunities for counterattacks. Sherman was flanking Johnston out of position after position, but up to this point in the campaign the Confederate general had perceived the opportunity for exactly one counterattack, the one McPherson referred to in the dispatch. Johnston was mistaken; the opportunity did not really exist; instead of being in maneuver McPherson was solidly dug in with his artillery planted for good fields of fire, and the Confederates took a stinging defeat.

Meanwhile Sherman had flanked the fortified defile at Allatoona; Johnston withdrew to the new line of hill country, where he had fortified, an event reported thus:

There have been few movements of importance in Georgia during the past week. On the 12th, General Sherman had his head-quarters at Big Shanty, with the lines of our army within 500 yards of the

The campaign in Georgia. Charge of Logan's troops at the Battle of Resaca,
May 14, 1864

enemy, who are posted along the hills from Kenesaw to Lost Mountain, protecting Marietta and the railroad south of that point.

Actually, there was a great deal more movement than the correspondent realized, and it was more important. He grasped the importance of Kenesaw Mountain and so did the artist; that was big and tangible in the background. But he missed completely the maneuvering accompanied by constant battle in which Sherman pinched out successive salients of the Confederate line at Pine Mountain, Gilgal Church, and Lost Mountain.

These were all trench lines, something which both correspondents and artists seem to have given no attention. Behind lay the bulk of Kenesaw Mountain, also entrenched, with the fortifications running far down to a deep muddy creek bearing the delightful name of Noses. This was the only time in the campaign that Sherman tried direct assault:

General Sherman's campaign. View of Kenesaw from Pine Mountain

General Sherman's advance. *Above:* Howard's XIV Corps crossing the Chattahoochee, July 12, 1864.
*Left:* Turner's Mill on Nickajack Creek, Georgia. *Right:* General Sherman's advance. Fish traps in the Chattahoochee

General Sherman's army is still confronted by the Kenesaw Mountain. The rainy weather and endangered communications have proved very annoying impediments. On Monday, June 27, Sherman attacked the enemy's position at Kenesaw Mountain, at the southwest end, at 8 A.M. While M'Pherson was engaged at this point, Thomas attacked at a point a mile further to the south; but the assault in both cases proved unsuccessful. M'Pherson's loss was about 500, and Thomas's 2000.

Again true and again overlooking an essential feature, which was not the fact that Lieutenant Ambrose Bierce was one of those wounded in the assault. The essential point was that while Thomas and McPherson were making their futile assault on Kenesaw, Schofield, the third army commander, had gained a foothold across Noses Creek. He developed the salient and shot some cavalry through to raid behind Johnston's lines.

Once again Johnston tried counterattack as a means of extricating himself, and once again the counterattack broke down, leaving the way open for a counter counterblow that broke right through the left of Johnston's lines. This made the Kenesaw position untenable; Johnston gave up both it and Marietta, the key city of this part of the campaign. The capture of Marietta was announced in the weeklies by quoting Sherman's dispatch.

This was in the issues of July 16; from this date forward to August 6 there was neither picture nor verbal coverage of Sherman's campaign. The gap is so curious as to invite a hunt for explanations. Sherman was having some trouble with his communications, that single line of railroad down from Chattanooga, which the rebel cavalry continually slashed at; but there was never any period of three weeks when they were cut, and his own dispatches to the War Department continued to flow.

Nor was there any lack of operations during the period. Kenesaw represented the last of the mountain barriers before Atlanta; the armies were in rolling, open country again, down to the Chattahoochee River, the last serious geographical barrier before Atlanta; and Sherman was maneuvering daily, with little spats of fighting. Yet anyone who depended on the weeklies for his information — and a good many people did — learned nothing of it.

Nor was this all. In mid-July Jefferson Davis became so dissatisfied with Johnston's constant retreats that he removed him in favor of John B. Hood, known as a fighting general. This meant battles and everyone on the Union as well as the Confederate side knew it, but there was neither dispatch nor editorial comment until some time later.

Colonel Jim Brownlow, an East Tennessean, caused an Incident by swimming the Chattahoochee naked with most of his regiment, falling on the Confederate picket posts and getting away with a number of men reported as 60, but probably less. After this, Confederate pickets were forbidden to talk to Yankees or to conduct the usual exchanges of newspapers for tobacco.

After the hiatus the running account of the war in Georgia goes on with a long narrative of the passage of the Chattahoochee, which was in fact, a very ably conducted piece of maneuver, and well told. The same dispatch continues:

On the 20th Hood came out and attacked Sherman's right, making three assaults, which "were bloodily repulsed"; the brunt of the assault fell on Hooker. The next day M'Pherson moved up to within two and a half miles of Atlanta, south and east, Blair's corps holding the extreme left, and reaching to within two miles of the Macon Railroad.

Colonel Brownlow on a picket hunt

This is the account of the Battle of Peachtree Creek, and as spot reporting it is a pretty poor one. The actual fact was that Sherman was trying a swinging approach on Atlanta from north and east, with McPherson on the outer end. Hood thought he saw a chance to break Thomas at the rear of the movement, and drove in to isolate him from the rest of the army. It was not Hooker's corps but those of Howard and Palmer that bore the brunt of the assault; one of Hooker's divisions arrived just as the last attack was being driven back. McPherson moved in that same day, not south and east but north and east; it was the menace of his advance that forced Hood to call off his attacks on Thomas and get back into the Atlanta trenches. Next comes:

Thursday our lines were pushed up close to the enemy's and part of Atlanta was in our possession. The next day, the 22d, Hood made another assault. The rebel army was chiefly massed against our right. The struggle ended with Hood's defeat, with a loss on our side of about 2500 and on that of the rebels of about 6000. General M'Pherson was shot while reconnoitering.

This is the tale of the Battle of Atlanta, and it is about as bad as the other. What happened was that Hood sent part of his force out by night to get behind the rear of Sherman's left (not his right) under McPherson, while the rest attacked the line in front and a cover attack was made against the Union center. McPherson was killed in the heat of battle while bringing up reinforcements.

Completely overlooked in the account was the fact that the men of Blair's corps had to jump over their entrenchments and fight them backward; also that it took Sherman in person with the reserve artillery to stabilize the situation. Completely overlooked also was the part of General John A. Logan, upon whom the cover attack at the center fell. He stopped it and then led a countercharge so severe that Hood called the whole battle off.

Logan was an interesting character who attracted a good deal of press attention, and one of the few strictly political generals to make a first-class record. He had some gift of inspirational leadership in battle; contemporary accounts and letters are full of the enthusiasm he engendered. Of himself he said: "Whatever I do in the heat of battle and on sudden inspiration is sure to be right; whatever I

John A. Logan in action

General Sherman's campaign. Battle of Ezra's Church (General Wood's division), July 28, 1864

do on mature deliberation is sure to be wrong." This was very nearly true and made him an outstanding corps commander, but not much good for anything above that.

Two weeks after the accounts given of Peachtree Creek and Atlanta, the weekly corrected its account of the former, principally, it would appear, from official dispatches and a congratulatory order issued by Thomas to his troops. A week later still it was talking about the third of the series of Atlanta battles, Ezra Church:

On the morning of the 28th the Army of the Tennessee was transferred to the extreme right, moving to within a short distance of the Macon road on the west of the city, the only railroad communication then left to the rebels. While this was transpiring Schofield, then holding the left, was attacked, having orders to refuse. As soon as Howard's army got into position (Army of the Tennessee), Stewart's rebel corps attacked him furiously with infantry and artillery. Loring's division of this rebel force attempted to flank Howard. This rebel column was, however, repulsed by Logan. The battle lasted till

five, no artillery being used by Howard, and very little by Stewart. Our forces had the advantage, as the enemy was wholly unprotected.

There is more of it, about some of the details of the action, but this is the main body. The interesting points are that the account is much longer and more detailed than those of the other battles, and a great deal more accurate. The reporter missed about the attack on Schofield; it was a feint, of which he should have been aware (Sherman was, at the time), and there was only one of Schofield's divisions involved. But all the rest checks with what has since been learned from reports and maps. Stewart did lead the attack just as Howard's advance got into position and began to build itself in; there was very little artillery employed, and Logan did prevent an attempt at envelopment; Confederate losses were very heavy, as stated.

The curious thing is how the verbal accounts of the campaign change abruptly from no reporting at all to inaccurate and incomplete reporting

217

The sinking of the *Alabama*, off Cherbourg, June 19, 1864

and then to full and accurate accounts. In a sense this reflects the feeling of the country — on both sides. By this date Grant and Lee were locked into immobility at Petersburg; there was no movement elsewhere; the elections were rushing on. "All now depends upon that army before Atlanta," people were writing.

Contemporary accounts and letters reflect a good deal of Northern fury over the operations of the Confederate sea raiders, usually referred to as "Anglo-rebel pirates"; and among the private letters of officers it is quite common to find expressed the hope that as soon as matters in the South were cleaned up, they would have a chance to make England pay. Nothing so much aroused the persistently expressed annoyance over Welles' admin-

istration of the Navy Department as the failure to catch these ships.

The fact was, of course, that Welles was in office during one of those difficult transition stages. Steam has vastly improved the speed of ships and the shell gun their striking power; but there had been no corresponding improvement in the means of communication, and when such a raider as *Alabama* put in at a port, the news had to come back to the United States by ship—by which time she was somewhere else. Nobody appears to have thought of convoys.

The meeting with *Kearsarge* off Cherbourg was thus largely accidental. It was decided by the better gunnery of the Union vessel; *Alabama's* crew were largely British-trained and concentrated on volume of fire rather than

*Left:* Before Petersburg. Carrying powder to the mine. *Right:* Colonel Pleasant superintending the arrival of the powder

accuracy. All this comes out very clearly indeed in the contemporary account, which is long, clear, and accurate, even including the presence of the British yacht which picked up many of the survivors.

It should be remembered that in that Black August of 1864 Lincoln himself did not believe he would be re-elected. After Cold Harbor and the crossing of the James, Grant closed around Petersburg, but despite his tenacity, the cautiousness of official expression, and what could be called the cheerfulness of press reports, it seemed evident that he was stopped—no progress. Now Sherman, after winning battles all across northern Georgia, was likewise whittled down to siege operations. The campaigns up the Red River, on the James, and in the Shenandoah Valley were failures. The Democrats had postponed their convention until the end of August to take advantage of what they expected would be more failures, and it seemed not impossible that they would have them.

For, aside from some obscure cavalry action south of the James and north of Richmond, the only real event at the main point of contact was the assault following the explosion of the Petersburg mine. Contemporary account:

For six weeks preparations had been making for a grand assault on the enemy's lines. The point to be gained was Cemetery Hill, a commanding position in regard to the other rebel fortifications. In order to break the centre of the rebel lines at this point, a battery of the rebels occupying a salient point was undermined. The mine was 400 feet long, with two galleries, and was charged with eight tons of powder. To divert Lee's attention to the north side of the James, operations were conducted on a large scale, threatening Richmond from General Foster's position at Deep Bottom. This led Lee to plant a force of from 15,000 to 20,000 north of the James.

Our lines on Saturday morning at 1 o'clock were disposed to suit the contemplated movement. The Ninth Corps held the centre, with the Eighteenth massed in the rear. Warren's (Fifth) Corps held the left in support. The signal for the assault was to be the explosion of the mine at 3½ o'clock, when a cannonade was to be opened from every cannon along the line, and the Ninth Corps was to charge through the gap laid open by the explosion.

If the mine had been exploded at the time set, the disposition and movement of our troops would have been covered in darkness; but there was a delay, and it was not till after light, at 4 o'clock and 40 minutes, that the signal was given, and the enemy was partially forewarned. The explosion was terrific; the battery (6 guns) was blown up, and a North Carolina regiment was buried in the chasm. Then the

219

artillery opened up all along the line and the charge was made, Ledlie's Division of Burnside's Corps in the advance. The Fourteenth New York Artillery were the first to enter the breach; seizing two of the rebel guns left in the ruins, these were turned against the enemy. The three assailing columns then pushed up toward the crest of the hill, but were driven back. Then the colored troops pressed up and broke. The rebel artillery slackened, and the enemy made a charge and were themselves repulsed. The assault was then given up.

This is another case where it is all true without telling the truth. The fact is that the business of "the Crater" as it came to be called, was one of the most mismanaged in the war. Nobody intended for the attacking columns to enter the big hole Colonel Pleasants had ingeniously blown in

the ground; the assault was to have gone in on both sides of it and work along, or into the rear of the Confederate trenches.

The arrangements had been carefully made at Meade's headquarters. Parapets were to have been built in the eight-foot-deep trenches on Burnside's front so the troops could mount rapidly, and engineer parties were detailed to get through the various obstructions on both sides. Burnside's headquarters did neither; when the big boom went off the men climbed painfully out of the trenches by sticking bayonets in the walls, and went straggling forward in ragged pairs and threes, not at all a line of attack. In addition, the covering cannonade was so heavy that the valley below Cemetery Hill quickly filled with smoke so that nobody could see what was going

General Grant's campaign. The charge on Cemetery Ridge, after the explosion, July 30, 1864

General Grant's campaign. Return of Kautz's cavalry expedition from its raid in Virginia

The offer of marriage refused

on; and to make everything perfect, General Ledlie, who was supposed to be leading the attack, stopped off in a bomb-proof to kill a bottle of rum with another general and was seen no more that day.

The consequence was that although the Confederates were considerably shocked and driven from most of the hill, there was no real Union attack, and most of the men who reached it slid down into the crater. It was soon packed with men who could not get out except backward, and the Confederates began to recover, then to shoot down into the crater. It was at this point that a division of colored troops was ordered forward. They did break; but they had adequate reason. They were being asked to climb through the trenches and obstacles in the face of an enemy fire that had now become intense.

Very little of this is in the contemporary press and the artists have

Army of the Potomac. General Stannard's headquarters

General Grant's campaign. In the trenches before Petersburg

RESOLVED,—THAT IN THE FUTURE, AS IN THE PAST, WE WILL ADHERE WITH UNSWERVING FIDELITY TO THE UNION UNDER THE CONSTITUTION, AS THE ONLY SOLID FOUNDATION OF OUR STRENGTH

THE CHIC

SECURITY, AND HAPPINESS AS A PEOPLE, AND AS A FRAME-WORK OF GOVERNMENT EQUALLY CONDUCIVE TO THE WELFARE AND PROSPERITY OF ALL THE STATES, BOTH NORTHERN AND SOUTHERN.

RESOLVED,—THAT THIS CONVENTION DO EXPLICITLY DECLARE, AS THE SENSE OF THE AMERICAN PEOPLE, THAT, AFTER FOUR YEARS OF FAILURE TO RESTORE THE UNION, B OF WAR, V DURING WHICH, UNDER THE PRETENSE OF A MILITARY NECESSI POWER HIGHER THAN THE CONSTITUTION

THE CONSTITUTION ITSELF HAS BEEN DISREGARDED

EVERY PART, AND PUBLIC LIBERTY AND PRIVATE RIGHT

ALIKE TRODDEN DOWN, AND THE MATERIAL PROSPERITY OF THE COUNTRY ESSENTIALLY IMPAIRED, JUSTICE, HUMANITY, LIBERTY,

GEORGE B. McCLELLAN

AND THE PUBLIC WELFARE, DEMAND THAT IMMEDIATE EFFORTS BE MADE FOR A CESSATION OF HOSTILITIES WITH A VIEW TO AN ULTIMATE CONVENTION OF ALL THE STATES

MEETING AT UNION SQUARE FOR PRESIDENT JEFF. DAVIS 1868.

OR OTHER PEACABLE MEANS TO THE END THAT AT THE EARLIEST PRACTICABLE MOMENT PEACE MAY BE RESTORED ON THE BASIS OF THE FEDERAL UNION OF THE STATES.

# PLATFORM.

RESOLVED, THAT THE DIRECT INTERFERENCE OF THE MILITARY AUTHORITY OF THE UNITED STATES IN THE RECENT ELECTIONS HELD IN KENTUCKY, MARYLAND, MISSOURI AND DELAWARE, WAS A SHAMEFUL VIOLATION OF THE CONSTITUTION,

THE OATH OF ALLEGIANCE MUST BE TAKEN BY ALL THE DISLOYAL CITIZENS. THE UNION MUST AND SHALL BE PRESERVED.

THE REPETITION OF SUCH ACTS IN THE APPROACHING ELECTION WILL BE HELD AS REVOLUTIONARY, AND RESISTED WITH ALL THE MEANS AND POWER UNDER OUR CONTROL.

FOR PRESIDENT.

RESOLVED, THAT THE AIM AND OBJECT OF THE DEMOCRATIC PARTY IS TO PRESERVE THE FEDERAL UNION AND THE RIGHTS OF THE STATES UNIMPAIRED, AND THEY HEREBY DECLARE

STATE RIGHTS AUCTION SALE SLAVES NIGGER DIED

THAT THEY CONSIDER THE ADMINISTRATIVE USURPATION OF EXTRAORDINARY AND DANGEROUS POWERS NOT GRANTED BY THE CONSTITUTION, THE SUBVERSION OF THE CIVIL BY MILITARY LAW IN STATES NOT IN INSURRECTION,

THE ARBITRARY MILITARY ARREST, IMPRISONMENT, TRIAL AND SENTENCE OF AMERICAN CITIZENS IN STATES WHERE CIVIL LAW EXISTS IN FULL FORCE, THE SUPPRESSION OF FREEDOM OF SPEECH AND OF THE PRESS, THE DENIAL OF THE RIGHT OF ASYLUM, THE OPEN AND AVOWED DISREGARD OF STATE RIGHTS

RESOLVED, THAT THEY WILL RECEIVE ALL THE CARE AND PROTECTION OF THE DEMOCRATIC PARTY, SYMPATHY, HUMANITY AND KINDNESS, LOVING POWER, THEY WILL RECEIVE ALL THE SYMPATHY OF THE DEMOCRATIC PARTY

AID AND COMFORT FOR REBELS TREASONABLE SPEECHES TRAITORS AT

THE EMPLOYMENT OF UNUSUAL TEST-OATHS, AND THE INTERFERENCE WITH AND DENIAL OF THE RIGHT OF THE PEOPLE TO BEAR ARMS, AS CALCULATED TO PREVENT A RESTORATION OF THE UNION AND THE PERPETUATION OF A GOVERNMENT DERIVING ITS JUST POWERS FROM THE CONSENT OF THE GOVERNED.

RESOLVED,—THAT THE SHAMEFUL DISREGARD OF THE ADMINISTRATION TO ITS DUTY IN RESPECT TO OUR FELLOW-CITIZENS WHO NOW AND LONG HAVE BEEN PRISONERS OF WAR IN A SUFFERING CONDITION, DESERVES THE SEVEREST REPROBATION, ON THE SCORE ALIKE OF PUBLIC INTEREST AND COMMON HUMANITY.

Th. Nast.

225

Farragut's fleet passing the forts and obstructions at the entrance of Mobile Bay, August 5, 1864: *Fort Morgan*, the monitors, *Hartford, Brooklyn, Richmond, Lackawanna, Monongahela, Ossipee*

The Rebel gunboat *Selma* surrendering to the United States steamer *Metacomet*

omitted the enshrouding smoke, which failed to make good pictures. About the only good results from the Crater were the dismissal of Ledlie and Burnside.

So the Democrats had a strong talking point for their Chicago convention. They nominated George B. McClellan, and adopted a platform that was summed up: "The war is a failure," but which contained a number of phrases that did not fail to attract the attention of the weeklies.

But the Chicago platform had hardly been announced—indeed it was still being written—when it began to receive destructive criticism, not so much from what the weeklies said as from the facts they chronicled.

The most cheering news of the week is that which comes to us from the Gulf. On Friday, August 5, Admiral Farragut with his fleet attacked the defense of Mobile and the rebel fleet in Mobile Bay. The report is from the rebel General Maury. He states that on the 5th Admiral Farragut with seventeen vessels—fourteen gun-boats and three monitors—passed Fort Morgan. The Monitor *Tecumseh* was sunk

by the guns of the fort. The rebel ram *Tennessee* surrendered after a desperate engagement in which Admiral Buchanan lost his leg, and was taken prisoner. Another rebel steamer, the *Selma*, was captured. Still another, the *Gaines*, was beached. The Federal fleet had approached the city.

This was the first flash report, and since it came through a Confederate source, it obviously could not include the facts that *Tecumseh* had fallen victim to a torpedo, or Farragut's famous: "Damn the torpedoes! Full speed ahead!" Indeed, the latter seems never to have made the contemporary press at all. But it did follow up:

The casualties on board the Federal fleet amounted to 129 killed and wounded. Twenty officers and one hundred and seventy men were captured on the rebel ram *Tennessee*. On the *Selma* were taken ninety officers and men.

On the morning of the 8th Fort Gaines surrendered unconditionally, with 56 officers, 848 enlisted men, its entire armament of 26 guns and a year's provisions. Fort Powell was deserted by its garrison, leaving 18 guns behind them. General Granger, in connection with the fleet, then

227

proceeded to the reduction of Fort Morgan.

The accompanying editorial does a little eagle-screaming, ending with: "Three cheers for the red, white, and blue." It rather curiously speaks of a "monitor controversy" and, without taking a definite stand, suggests that a good many people doubt the value of this class of vessels. The returns from eyewitnesses on that part of the front were evidently not all in yet: Farragut had refused to enter the bay and take on *Tennessee* at all until he had some monitors, and in the battle it was Perkins' *Chickasaw*, hanging under the ram's stern and pounding her with 11-inch till she could neither steam nor steer, that did the business.

The picture coverage was extremely good. It is doubtful whether Farragut's wooden ships were ever in such a precise line as is represented; *Brooklyn* was leading it, and it was not until the old man shouted his famous command that his flagship shoved past her. Also, the ocean-going ships were stripped down to topmasts, as is clearly visible in the picture of the grapple between *Richmond* and *Tennessee*. But the rest is all real enough and probably, in view of the accuracy of detail about *Metacomet* and *Selma*, rather unusual vessels, from the hand of an eyewitness.

*Selma* tried to get away up the bay after Farragut had passed the forts, and *Metacomet* was sent in chase of her; the curious fact being that although the latter was a side-wheeler and a double-ender, she was the fastest ship in Farragut's fleet. A curious incident of that action deserves retelling. Captain Jouett of the Union craft and Captain Murphy of the Confederate had been good pre-war friends. When the latter was taken aboard *Metacomet* as a prisoner, he found a table laid and on it cold lobsters, his favorite dish.

There was something wrong with nearly all the rebel rams, and in the case of *Tennessee*, as the artist who drew the picture remarks, it was her

The United States steamer *Richmond* engaging the Rebel ram *Tennessee*, August 5, 1864

The campaign in Georgia. A baggage train crossing the mountains in a storm

229

Paris fashions for September, 1864

Crow's-nest signal station

port shutters. They were subject to jamming when struck hard, and at Mobile Bay, two of them jammed so they could not be opened, while a third was shot away, and through the gap thus left a shell entered which wounded the admiral and did considerable internal damage.

Mr. Gideon Welles felt "a blight of sadness like a dark shadow," and the Chicago convention finished its deliberations and nominated McClellan amid vast enthusiasm on August 31. But on September 3, waiting for daylight in the War Department, Lincoln was handed a dispatch that ended in electric words:

> Atlanta is ours and fairly won.
> W. T. Sherman

The news coverage was good:

Sherman had removed his army from Atlanta during the last week of August,

General Sherman's army destroying the Macon railroad between Rough and Ready and Jonesborough, Georgia

and transferred it to a position on the West Point Road, from which an advance was made upon the Macon Road in three columns — one under Howard, who was to strike the road near Jonesborough on the right; another under Schofield, whose goal was Rough and Ready on the left; while the third column, under Thomas, pushed up to the road at Conche's in the centre. A part of Hood's army occupying Jonesborough was thus cut off from the main force at Atlanta. This detachment attacked Howard, who had intrenched himself on the road north of Jonesborough, but were easily repulsed. The whole army advanced upon the road, and destroyed it between Jonesborough and Rough and Ready; and on the 1st of September Jefferson C. Davis, commanding the Fourteenth Corps, attacked and carried the rebel works at Jonesborough, capturing 10 guns and 1000 prisoners. The defeated rebels moved south to Lovejoy's Station, and were pursued. In the meantime Hood blew up his magazines at Atlanta, and evacuated that important position by night. Atlanta was immediately occupied by General Slocum, commanding the Twentieth Corps.

The only thing lacking in this account is the fact that Sherman cut loose from his communications to make the sweep south of Atlanta, like Grant in the Vicksburg campaign; but the whole matter of communications was rather consistently neglected by front-line reporters throughout the war.

The editorial treatment of the victory also hit the nail pretty squarely on the head:

There is not a man who does not feel that M'Clellan's chances were diminished by the glad tidings from Atlanta; nor any one who does not know that if Sherman had been defeated, the friends of the Chicago candidate would have felt surer of his success. When people solemnly resolve, as the party which has nominated General M'Clellan at Chicago, that "the experiment of war" to maintain the Government and restore the Union is a "failure," how can they be glad to hear of a great and vital victory which belies their theory? No unconditional Union man could have asked a more significant commentary upon the true character of the Chicago movement. For suppose the great M'Clellan ratification meeting had taken place upon the Saturday the news of Sherman's glorious victory was received, how like a soaking storm it would have fallen upon an assembly whose cardinal principle is a "demand that immediate efforts be made for a cessation of hostilities!" Sherman has done more, in his capture of Atlanta, for a cessation of hostilities than Vallandigham and his Convention could do in twelve months of abuse of the Administration.

And elsewhere:

Surely we may rejoice that we have emerged from the dark days of doubt and inefficiency. Surely we may offer thanksgiving that the great armies of the American Union are now commanded by leaders who are not only the most skillful, daring, rapid, tenacious of soldiers—whom neither mud nor Quaker guns appall—but also men who are devoted in every fibre

231

Rebels moving south from Atlanta

The halt

General Grant's campaign. *Above:* Captain Ashby's New York battery in the trenches before Petersburg. *Middle:* The gunners of the XVIII Corps protected by Mantelets. *Below:* Shelling the enemy from the Cohorns

The Rebels destroying the Chesapeake and Ohio Canal

of their frames and drop of their blood to the faith that the experiment of war to restore the Union is *not* a failure; and that no other effort for the immediate cessation of hostilities should be made by the loyal American people except renewed and overwhelming vigor in the war to confirm the absolute supremacy of the Government.

The fall of Atlanta came so soon after the nomination that McClellan had to issue his letter of acceptance after the news, and he and his advisers were forced into some remarkable wriggling about that platform. This also came in for some editorial analysis:

The ruins of Chambersburg. Bank and Franklin Hotel

Sheridan's campaign. Battle of Winchester. Position of the XIX Corps, General Emery, September 19. The center

He declares that the war ought to have been prosecuted only to maintain the Union. No man knows better than he that it never has been prosecuted for any other purpose, nor has any authorized person ever announced any other. When General M'Clellan bagged the entire Legislature of Maryland it was done to maintain the Union. When his friend Vallandigham was arrested it was for the same purpose. When the emancipation proclamation was issued it was for the same result.

He says that when "our present adversaries"—meaning the rebels—clearly want peace "upon the basis of the Union," they ought to have it. Yes, and they will have it. The only basis of the Union is the Constitution. When the rebels submit to that, they will have peace of course. Nobody ever said otherwise except those who nominated General M'Clellan.

He says:

"If a frank, earnest and persistent effort to obtain these objects should fail, the responsibility for ulterior consequences will fall upon those who remain in arms against the Union. But the Union must be preserved at all hazards."

The General's political strategy is no better than his military.

Lee himself had expressed the opinion that if the Army of the Potomac reached the James it would become only a question of time; and the army was there. But there was still a device that might work; the old one of 1862, when Stonewall Jackson had set so many plans awry by a campaign down the Shenandoah

Valley and a threat to Washington. This was how the Union began to have Early trouble. The first report was:

General Early, who was sent against Hunter in the Shenandoah, not being able to compel an engagement, marched northward in the direction of Martinsburg, threatening a raid across the Potomac. General Sigel fell back forthwith from Shepardstown to Maryland Heights. Rebel forces have been reported at Williamsport, Falling Waters, Hagerstown and other places, but the only force which at the latest advices were known to have crossed the Potomac are about 2500 cavalry under General Ransom and 5000 infantry under Early.

This is very bad reporting indeed; Early had defeated Sigel and driven Hunter's West Virginia army back into the passes with the loss of its wagons and stores. The fact that Early now came down through Maryland to defeat a scratch force under Lew Wallace at the Monocacy and pushed on until he was in sight of the Capitol was not reported at all, and the second raid in which Early burned Chambersburg got only a single line as a pendant to a report of a minor engagement with Crook's VIII Corps in the valley.

The valley operations were treated as something to sweep under a rug; the Confederates had always won there and presumably always would,

The cavalry charge at Winchester, Virginia, September 19, 1864

Sheridan's army on the march up the Shenandoah Valley

and there was not even good picture coverage. Then comes a brief note:

"General Hunter has been superseded by General Sheridan in the Department of the Shenandoah. The rebels have appeared in large force at various points along the Potomac."

This was in the August of discontent; in September, Sheridan was reported (erroneously) to have lost a battle and to be falling back. Later in the same month Early "disappeared from Sheridan's front," then reappeared, and there are reports of skirmishes which in fact took place. It was still unimportant. But toward the end of September came an event that got more space than the operations of any other army—Sheridan had attacked at the Opequon and won a ringing, a sensational, victory.

It was 3 o'clock P.M. General Crook had formed on Sheridan's right and rear. The Federal line, three miles long, then advanced under cover of a tremendous artillery fire; and shortly after this advance the cavalry on the right were led by their masterly leaders in an impetuous charge which broke the ranks of the rebel army.

It is hard to convey to any modern reader the sense of delight caused by this extraordinary news. The victory had been won over a general who had come within sight of Washington and who, at that date, bore at least as high a name as Jackson in the days of his triumphs; it had been won in the valley, that pocket borough of the Confederacy; and the decisive stroke had been a stormy charge of cavalry, the arm in which the Confederates were always previously superior. There was more to come:

On the 22d the rebels were found posted in an almost impregnable position, at Fisher's hill, about three miles beyond Strasburg, and at about four o'clock in the evening the attack on their lines was made, Gen. Crook furiously attacking them on their left, resting on North mountain, and the 6th and 19th corps in front. Crook carried everything before him, his men driving the rebels in confusion and sweeping down behind their breastworks. The attack of the 6th and 19th corps was equally effective. Our army captured 16 pieces of artillery and a great many caissons, artillery horses, &c. Gen. Sheridan was pushing up the valley so rapidly that

238

he was unable to tell his own or the rebel losses, or to state the number of prisoners he had captured. He says: "Only darkness has saved the whole of Early's army from destruction."

The account is a good deal sketchier than those the reporters had learned to give to a public which was beginning to understand military maneuver. It also omits the important feature of the means by which Sheridan won his victory. The Confederates had dug themselves in with a ravine in front and their wings resting on two mountains; Sheridan sent the whole VIII Corps around one of them with guns wrapped in rags to hide the gleam, and just at twilight released them for the attack on the flank and rear of Early's army. It was no wonder that Crook carried everything before him.

Fisher's Hill confirmed Winchester (or the Opequon, as it was later called) and proved that the first victory had been no accident. Even at the time the sense of its moral and physical significance was widespread. Lincoln telegraphed: "God bless you, one and all"; Grant ordered hundred-gun salutes fired from all the batteries before Petersburg, and George Ticknor in Boston noticed total strangers shaking hands on the street in mutual congratulation.

Although the Battle of the Opequon was given extensive pictorial coverage, that at Fisher's Hill, oddly enough, received almost none at all. Sheridan personally received most of it, usually represented as a solitary figure out of deference to his lack of height, to which he was supposed (falsely) to be sensitive.

On October 15, 1864, a little group of men who had seeped into St. Albans, Vermont, from Canada by ones and twos, suddenly appeared in the streets. They were Confederate soldiers led by Lieutenant Bennett Young, and they proceeded to rob the bank of all the gold it contained and set fire to several buildings, beside making a couple of prominent locals take an oath to the Confederacy.

Night after the battle

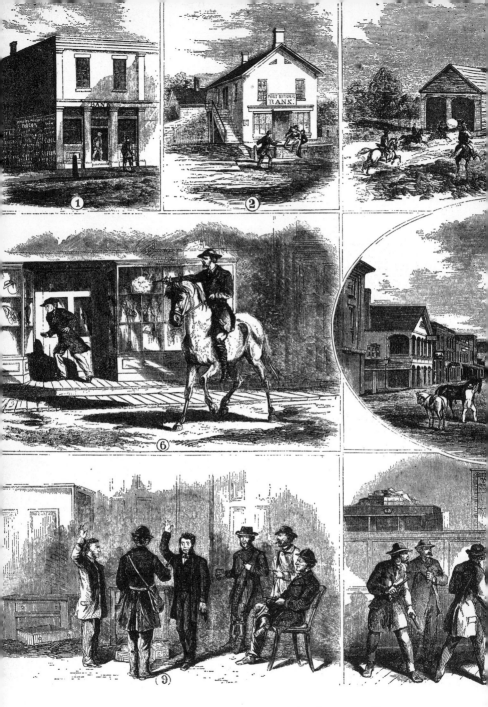

Raid on St. Albans, Vermont, by

Rebels from Canada, on October 19

Sheridan's ride

There was some resistance on the part of citizens who got their own guns out, and a number · of persons never actually determined, but probably not above five, were shot. Nearly all the raiders got away in spite of the efforts of a posse which turned out rapidly to follow them.

The affair made an immense sensation at the time and on demand of Secretary Seward the raiders were apprehended and tried in a Canadian civil court on charges of arson, robbery, and treason. They won an acquittal on the grounds that they had performed a legitimate act of war; but this did not turn out so well for the Canadian authorities, who were stuck with an international case for allowing neutrality to be violated, and had to pay damages.

Confederate agent George Sanders, who organized the raid but did not go on it himself, became a great local hero in Montreal and was frequently observed in hotels there, "surrounded by oysters and women."

The Battle of Cedar Creek was liberally reported in the stirring stanzas of Thomas Buchanan Read, which were out almost as soon as it was over; but even the baldest prose narrative carried a thrill:

The General was in Winchester in the early morning when the enemy attacked.

The enemy had approached under cover of a heavy fog, and flanking the extreme right of the Federal lines, had thrown the entire line into confusion, and driven it several miles. The stragglers to the rear were fearfully numerous, and the enemy was pushing on, turning against the Federals a score of guns already captured from them.

This was the situation a little before noon when Sheridan came on the field. A staff-officer meeting him pronounced the situation of the army to be "awful."

"Pshaw," said Sheridan, "it's nothing of the sort. It's all right, or we'll fix it right!"

Galloping past the batteries to the extreme left of the line held by the cavalry, he rode to the front, took off his hat and waved it, while a cheer went up from the ranks. Generals rode out to meet him, officers waved their swords, men threw up their hats in an extremity of glee.

Behind him the stragglers of the army defeated in the morning were pouring back to the front, slapping their musket butts and shouting, "Sheridan!"

The line was speedily re-formed. An attack just about to be made was repulsed and the tide of battle turned. A cavalry charge was ordered against right and left flank of the enemy, and then a grand advance of the three infantry corps from left to right on the enemy's centre. On through Middletown and beyond the enemy hurried, and the Army of the Shenandoah pursued. The roar of musketry now had a gleeful, dancing sound. The guns fired shotted salutes of victory.

Two thousand prisoners were gathered together. The guns lost in the morning were recaptured, and as many more taken, and the enemy reached Mount Jackson without an organized regiment.

The scene at Sheridan's head-quarters at night was wildly exciting. General Custer arrived about 9 o'clock. The first thing he did was to hug General Sheridan with all his might, lifting him in the air, with the shout: "By ——, we've cleaned them out and got the guns!"

No victory in the war produced a greater effect than Cedar Creek, not even Mobile or Atlanta or Sheridan's earlier successes in the valley. The press would not let it alone, and the pro-Lincoln politicians would not either; it was the perfect piece of campaign material, and with reason. Not only was it the latest number in a series which demonstrated unquestionably that the war was not a failure, but could go on from victory to victory. It was also in some sense an epitome of the war itself, the North rallying after apparently hopeless defeat to clean them out and get the guns. And it also provided the North with a figure hitherto lacking, a dashing whirlwind of a man whose mere presence changed everything. "My, my, this is good news indeed,"

Cedar Creek. The Union attack after the rally

Destruction of the Rebel ram *Albemarle,* on the Roanoke River, on the night of October 27, by a torpedo boat, under command of Lieutenant William B. Cushing, U.S.N.

said Lincoln. "This Sheridan is a little Irishman, but he is a big fighter."

After Cedar Creek the election was hardly any longer in doubt. Lincoln, who in August had thought it probable that he would not be re-elected, penciled a new memorandum before the battle, showing himself winner by three electoral votes, but forgetting the three of Nevada. He made no predictions after Cedar Creek, but his secretaries noticed that his step was springier, and he clearly must have felt a good deal better about the prospects.

Just before the election itself there was more good news. *Albemarle,* the dragon ship of the Carolina sounds, had been destroyed by a young lieutenant named William B. Cushing. He took a little launch of 13 men in, a spar torpedo in her bow, and found her anchored in the Roanoke River, with a big boom of logs around her. It was impenetrable; he drove his launch at the boom, rode over it, and fired the torpedo that sank the ram just as she fired a shot that sank the launch.

Cushing himself was the only survivor who escaped, all the rest captured. Both the verbal and pictorial reporting, which were extraordinarily prompt, must have come from him. The curious feature about it is that both weeklies had good and full ver-

bal accounts, but *Leslie's,* in the picture reproduced here, was the only one that got anything like a true picture. The *Harper's* drawing shows an ironclad going up to a sharp peak, no upper deck at all. This seems to have been something of a mania, or delusion, with *Harper's* artists, the ones who did it being nowhere given names; time and again they pictured the rebel rams that way, even including *Manassas* at New Orleans, which was a turtle-back and so reported in the accompanying copy.

Contemporary copy as to the election in New York City, where much trouble was feared (memory of the draft riots) and none whatever occurred:

The enterprise of the press was well illustrated at the *Herald* office, where the returns were displayed to an anxious and agitated crowd by means of a calcium light. We have not space to give to a tithe of the amusing dialogues heard *membra disjecta.* The confusion of Babel is a faint type of the multitudinous gabble of the surrounding crowd. It was, however, clear that "Little Mac" was the undoubted favorite, although many a remark about gunboats was heard, and that he was more of a naval than a military hero.

There was no other pictorial coverage of the election than the one given here; the verbal coverage was limited to editorials saying substantially what the historians have said: that by a vote in which McClellan carried only three states and had a ten-to-one minority in the electoral college, the nation had overwhelmingly given its confidence to Lincoln.

There is something rather curious here. At about 7:30 P.M. the President went over to the War Department through wind and rain to hear the returns, because it had the best telegraph in Washington. He sat around talking all evening, telling stories which progressively became gayer as the news came in, piece by piece, that Maryland had unexpectedly gone for the Union and even in New York City, Henry Raymond had carried a solid Democratic constituency for the Union party.

There are several narratives of the scene, including one of the President helping shovel out fried oysters at midnight, while the rain ceased, the worst of the storm over, crowds began to march down the avenue, singing

Night scene at the N.Y. *Herald* office. Displaying election returns by means of a calcium light

"The Battle Cry of Freedom." Not a trace of this in the contemporary accounts; yet the newspaper men were not excluded, and some of the tales come from them. A mystery of 1864 journalism.

Process of cooking 2000 turkeys for soldiers' Thanksgiving dinner

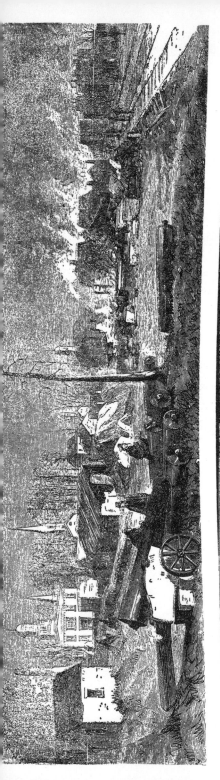

*Above:* Destruction of the depots, public buildings, and manufactories at Atlanta, Georgia, November 15, 1864. *Below:* The XIV and XX Corps moving out of Atlanta, November 15

On November 15, 1864, Sherman burned Atlanta, or everything of military importance in it (viewpoints differ) and set off on that march through Georgia which became the subject of the best American war song ever written. He had no communications, and for the first time in the war this became visible and audible to the press. Lincoln was anxious as the Southern papers talked about Napoleon's plunge into Russia; Grant, who had been brought round to sanctioning the expedition, asked merely where the Confederates were going to get their winter. The weekly press was frank about its inadequacy:

The news from Sheridan is still indefinite; indeed it is very apparent that the rebel journals are unable to locate his main army with any degree of accuracy. The Mayor of Milledgeville says that the Yankee army has despoiled the citizens of food, and has taken their mules and horses. He also reports the destruction of the railroad bridge and the bridge across the Oconee. The State House and Executive Mansion were uninjured. There is no certain indication that Sherman has moved his main army east of the Oconee, though there were rumors of his having reached Millen. The Richmond *Enquirer* of December 1, on the basis of the report that Sherman had reached Millen, declared its opinion that he would reach the coast in safety. The Richmond *Examiner,*

The Aesthetico-Neuralgicon

two days afterward, denied the report and predicted Sherman's defeat.

This is accompanied by editorial speculation and warning, preparing the public in case things have gone wrong:

We shall be very glad if we can contribute in any degree to promote a healthful condition of the public mind, guarding it against mad ecstasies and foolish depressions. The cause is not gained or lost by a battle nor by a campaign. The noblest causes defended by arms, can not have a campaign of unvarying success; and a nation which can not endure occasional defeat can not achieve permanent victory."

The Aesthetico-Neuralgicon was the big medical discovery of that winter. It was an outgrowth of the homeopathic system of medicine and was intended to introduce medicaments into every tissue (through the nose) and cure everything.

The Battle of Franklin, in which Hood was so severely checked on his adventure back into Tennessee, received very little verbal coverage and no picture coverage at all, in spite of the fact that it was a much more severe action than many that had gone earlier.

Nashville was another story; it got picture coverage of a rather conventional sort, but a convention now fairly well informed by observation, and verbal coverage that affords some interest as of today:

On Monday, 15th Dec., the Union army under Gen. Thomas attacked the rebels under Gen. Hood, and after a severe action of nine hours, drove them three miles back, capturing several miles of their earthworks, 800 prisoners, and seven guns. The next morning Gen. Thomas renewed the attack, and drove their left from the Cumberland River, forcing them back about six miles. At this point the gunboats came into play, and did excellent service. All Hood's earthworks throughout the entire extent of his lines, except about a mile on his right, were captured. Thomas has captured over 1000 prisoners and 16 guns. Hood's whole army of 50,000 men was engaged, and is said to be utterly routed and cut to pieces.

Charge of 3rd Brigade, 1st Division, XVI Corps, at the Battle of Nashville, Tennessee, December 15, 1864

The Union Army entered Savannah on December 21, and on the 24th the first number of the *Loyal Georgian* was issued

This is clearly the account of a victory, which readers may discount as regards the last sentence, the sort of thing that had been reported many times before. It is possible that the reporters had been told the real facts and did so discount. They could hardly have been out at the fringes of the advance with Wilson's cavalry and seen what actually happened in the prone route of Hood's army. For the prisoners were not 1000, as reported by the press, but 10,000, an absolutely incredible figure for a battle (more had been taken in sieges), and Hood's army was so utterly crushed that of over 44,000 men with whom he began the campaign, he could rally only 9000 behind the Duck River. The loss in guns was not 16 but 72; the gunboats never had anything to do with the battle.

In other words, the reporters completely missed the big news of the day, and some of the biggest of the war.

The tension about Sherman's march grew because there was no news at all except that which came through Confederate sources, uncertain and unfriendly. Most of the Northern press did not even reprint such pickups as: "Sherman's men are starving. The Georgians have risen and are shooting the Yankees down at every crossroad. Five thousand prisoners from Sherman's army arrived here yesterday. He has barely a division left."

Under such rumors the dailies became nervous; the weeklies kept repeating their assurances that a lost battle was not a lost war. But as of Christmas Eve there was a dispatch in all newspaper offices, transmitted by ship from the South:

Savannah, Ga., Dec. 22, 1864
His Excellency President Lincoln:
I beg to present you as a Christmas gift the city of Savannah, with 150 heavy guns and plenty of ammunition, and also about 25,000 bales of cotton.
W. T. Sherman

The assault and capture of Fort Fisher, January 15, 1865

It was as sensational as the news from Atlanta and, like that, was appreciated at full value. *Harper's* editorialized:

This is the triumphant completion of a campaign which, at its beginning, every one must have felt to be daring and dangerous, and which, seen from Europe, appeared in its just proportions as one of the great military movements of modern times. Its success was clearly seen to be the proof of fatal weakness in the rebel section and to foretell the doom of the rebellion — and it has succeeded. It is a success which can not be extenuated or explained away. General Sherman and his army moved from Chattanooga to Atlanta because neither Johnston, nor Hood, nor Jefferson Davis, nor the rebel confederacy could help themselves. And Sherman and his men made "an agreeable march" from Atlanta to Savannah because the people of Georgia did not care to help themselves.

All true; it may be added only that the pictorial coverage of the march through Georgia was non-existent, and Sherman's appearance at Savannah was pictured only by artists with the fleet.

The winter of 1862-63 was one of discontent; every success was canceled by a failure. That of 1863-64 was a waiting winter in which the war went to sleep from mid-November to May. The winter of 1864-65 was entirely different; there was a show going on in every ring of the circus and all the time. The election, Sherman's march, the Battle of Nashville, Sherman's arrival at Savannah followed close; and on their heels there came the fitting out of a great naval expedition which could only have one object: the entrances to Wilmington, the last great port still open to the Confederacy.

250

The fleet of Admiral Porter was the largest ever assembled under the American flag, and there were 7000 troops under Ben Butler. Contemporary accounts make no bones about the terrible fiasco that ensued after a shipload of powder arranged by Butler blew up off the fort and failed to shake it in the least; the ships moved in for a bombardment and the troops were landed. Butler refused to assault; the troops were taken aboard again, and on his return Grant promptly removed him in spite of his potent political influence.

The press commented acidly on his farewell order to the troops: "I have refused to order the sacrifices of such soldiers; and I am relieved of command," and gave a review of his military career, saying very frankly that his campaign at the head of the Army of the James was a failure.

But even as the weeklies were offering this comment on Butler, word came through that the expedition had returned to Fort Fisher under A. H. Terry and taken the place by assault with the help of close-in naval bombardment. The event received unusually good verbal coverage, with a detailed account of the attempt of the fleet marines to storm the sea face of the fort, and a careful narrative of how the successive parallels were taken. The picture coverage was less good, although there seem to have been artists with the expedition. The drawing showing the storm of the fort goes back to the old convention of men all in line and shoulder to shoulder.

There has never been a campaign quite like that of Sherman through the Carolinas and its impact was fully appreciated at the time:

Bounty-jumpers' parade, at Indianapolis, Indiana: superintended by Colonel Warner

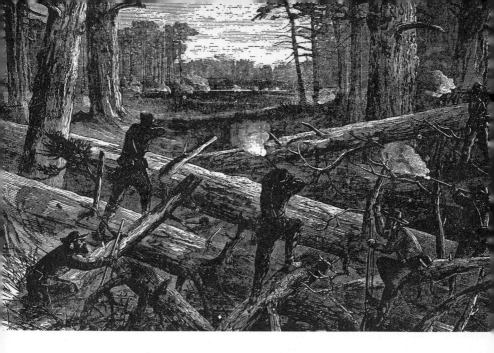

Sherman's march through South Carolina. Road at the swamp crossings

Sherman has exposed the mask and the brag of the rebellion. Rebel gascons will boast, but he has taught us the exact value of gasconade. "Sherman will find a lion in his path," says the Richmond *Examiner,* "Beauregard is in his front." "Long before Columbia falls," says the Columbia *Carolinian* of February 12, "we look for a battle and a victory commensurate in its consequences with the great interests now at stake, one which will prove that 'God is fighting by our side, although with visor down,' and that he has vouchsafed to Carolina the proud privilege of closing as she began the war—in triumph." Five days afterward Columbia was occupied by Sherman. The lion Beauregard stole away; and the ludicrous newspaper, which asked "what reason is there to anticipate an immediate advance upon Columbia: we can recall none, to believe it is contrary to common sense," had no sooner spoken than Sherman arrived.

This was the psychological impact; but the editors missed something the artists completely caught—to wit, the true nature of the campaign. For it was not Beauregard or Southern soldiers who provided the real opposition; it was the Carolina country, heavily wooded, filled with swamps crossed by slow streams, now full with spring. "That's the kind of country we'll catch the Yankees in," said a Carolina planter to English correspondent Russell in the first year of the war, with a wave of the hand.

Well, they had caught the Yankees in it and the drawings attest what kind of country it was. But these Yankees were mostly Northwesterners, farmers and woodsmen used to doing everything. There were no roads; they chopped down the trees and made them. There were no bridges; they built them. The Salkahatchie has 15 channels in the swamps that bear its name; 15 bridges were built over them in a single day. The Edisto is half a mile wide where the army struck it;

Sherman's march through South Carolina. Advance from M'Phersonville, February 1, 1865

Howard's wing crossed it in four hours, with wagons and artillery.

Sherman's push through the Carolinas, 16 days from Savannah to Columbia, has always been regarded by military men as one of the greatest marches of history. At the time it was accepted as a normal event, however; it was only the psychological impact that counted. The burning of Colum-

The Rebel attack on Fort Steadman, March 25, 1865

General Sheridan at the Battle of Five Forks, April 1, 1865

bia was not even reported until the Southern papers made a fuss about it.

Lee comprehended fully the significance of Sherman's rush through the Carolinas, but there is no sign that the press understood the meaning of Lee's desperate attempt to disengage at Petersburg by striking through Fort Steadman at Grant's base of supplies. The attack was reported only in the official dispatch of General Parke, on whose corps it fell, and even so was accorded little space.

Grant, if nobody else, understood the full importance of what had happened and began that last shift to his left which resulted in the Battle of Five Forks and then the evacuation of Richmond as a result of the capture of Petersburg following hard on that battle. The press was caught com-

pletely by surprise by Five Forks, the assault on Petersburg that followed, the evacuation of Richmond, Sailor's Creek, and the pursuit of Lee that ended at Appomattox. Fort Steadman was reported pictorially, but later. Five Forks was hardly reported at all until the memoirs began to come out. At the time *Harper's* said only:

"The result of the series of battles beginning March 29 and ending April 2 can hardly be estimated with any degree of accuracy."

The picture coverage of the battles that led to the end of the war was quite as poor. Sheridan is shown wearing a beard longer than he ever wore, riding a horse which is doing the conventional belly-gallop, and waving a sword. There are eye-witness accounts of what he did at Five Forks; he did lead the final victorious charge on horseback, but he was waving a flag, not a sword, and he had no hat on. In short, the pictorial reporting was pure imagination and not even an informed imagination.

The editorial columns were no better. They were busy that week discussing our relations with England, the question of whether or not the President should offer an amnesty in return for Confederate surrender, the fate of the son of Dr. Livingstone of Africa, and corruption in the New York legislature.

Sailor's Creek, where Lee's army was broken in half during the retreat from Richmond, received neither verbal nor pictorial reporting. It is simply ignored as part of the series of battles.

Lee's surrender was reported very quietly:

Upon the evacuation of Richmond and Petersburg Lee's army moved westward toward Burkesville. The army was thoroughly demoralized, and the line of retreat was strewn with muskets, knapsacks, and artillery caisson. General Grant distinguished himself in the pursuit no less notably than in the defeat of the rebels. Moving his own army westward, he kept pushing Lee northward, keeping him to the north bank of the Appomattox. Lee fianlly succeeded in crossing the river and concentrated his army in the region of Amelia Court House. But in the mean while, by the night of Tuesday, April 4, Sheridan and the Fifth Corps had, by a march of thirty-six miles, gained a position west of Lee, near Jettersville, on the road to Burkesville.

The Union army entering Richmond, April 3, 1865

Grant, on Wednesday with the Twenty-fourth Corps, had reached Nottaway Court House, and here learned that Lee had been intercepted. On Thursday Grant had brought his army up to Sheridan's support, and with the Second, Fifth and Sixth Corps lay in line of battle at Burke's Station, facing to the north and cutting Lee off.

There follows a brief narrative of the exchange of notes between the two generals, ending with:

General,—I have received your letter of this date, containing the terms of surrender of the Army of Northern Virginia by you. As they are substantially the same as those expressed in your letter of the 8th instant, they are accepted. I will proceed to designate the proper officers to carry the stipulations into effect.

Very respectfully your obedient
servant,
R. E. Lee, General.

All the surrender pictures are much after the event. The fact is that during that last week of the war, things moved too fast, and the assassination of Lincoln followed so quickly that the pictorial reporters never caught up.

Grand review of the National armies at Washington, May 24, 1865